Organic Marketing™

A Guide to Defining
Your Certain Way

Allan Curtis
Sandi Maki

Acknowledgements of Awesomeness

As we began looking toward the future for our "Ask the Pool Guy" brand, we summed up our mission with these words: *Happy Pools. Happy Customers. Happy Pool Guy.*

This became the basis for all of our business decisions, customer service policies, and marketing efforts. We discovered if the pools we serviced could be happy, then our customers would be happy, and our team (and Pool Guy) could be happy as well.

Thank you to our awesome customers who work with us and continue to choose us—we wouldn't be where we are without you.

Thank you to our team members who help create such a great customer experience and such a great team to work every single day!

Finally, ***thank you to our leader***, the one and only Pool Guy, who has helped to create such a wonderful, nurturing, inspiring, innovative and fun work environment. It's amazing that we can all be a part of something so extraordinary.[1]
—Sandi Maki

---

[1] "Thank you," Sandi, for engaging everyone and truly being the coordinator of everything. This book would not exist without you.

As you read this book, you'll notice it's written from our two different perspectives. You may notice each of our voices throughout. You can have fun figuring out who is who, or just read through and have a great time discovering the philosophies and how to apply them in your life and business. Thanks for coming on this journey with us. —Al and Sandi

---

Organic Marketing ™

Contents

Introduction

Thoughts from Sandi: It was 20 years ago when Al Curtis, "Ask the Pool Guy," became the owner of a swimming pool construction/service company. At the age of 26, Al already had seven years of experience in the business and was technically skilled at the work, but was woefully unequipped to handle the business end of things.

By sheer grit and determination, Al said "yes" to most anything, handling every lead and trying to turn every phone call into revenue. Customer service was disorganized, and the crews ran from job to job based on who was complaining the loudest.

It was no way to run a business, let alone create long term satisfaction. A few years in, and Al had managed to put together some solid and friendly crews, and the business was doing okay. There was still something lacking; there was no "special something" that set Al's company apart from any other competitor in his market.

After nearly a decade of this, Al was ready to let it go and try something new. Around this same time, I came in as a partner, through a series of coincidences that seem improbable in hindsight. We continued to work to grow the company for a few years, then decided to step away from the pool business for a while and create InSights Group, a business networking community of like-minded people all focused on finding "a better way" to work, to live and to be happy.

Then something funny happened. Turning our attention away from the pool business allowed Al to set aside everything he knew and felt about it. In doing this, he found that he truly did love the work he was doing; he just needed to find a new way do the work. A new way that would be more manageable, more profitable, and yes, more fun.

We began asking ourselves *what if? What if* we could build a company strictly doing the work we loved to do?

We decided that this was the new path we would take. We didn't have a map, so we invented one. Through our process that came to be known as Organic Marketing™ we began to discover how all the pieces of this new way of doing business could work together.

We started with our Why and followed this as the Guide to Defining **Our Certain Way**. This book you are reading outlines our journey.

Preface

We have been avid students of the philosophy of Wallace D. Wattles and his book *The Science of Getting Rich*. Through our exploration of his writings, we began to create our version of *Our Certain Way.*

> *"Success is becoming what you want to be, and is attained by applying your energies to your work, and you will apply your energies in exact proportion to the intensity of your desire."—Wallace Wattles*

How to Promote Yourself

What we have found is that applying our thoughts about Our Certain Way to what we are doing creates change almost immediately.

Opportunities that we started to think about began to almost effortlessly come our way.

The action part of developing **Your Certain Way** is creating the crystal clear vision of what you want. Next is the concentrated effort you will put forth in that direction and the finally the faith and persistence to see it through.

"The intensity of your desire will depend on the clearness of which you picture to yourself what you want to be." —Wallace Wattles

The Organic Marketing™ Process that we outline through this manuscript helps you to go through the discovery for yourself to begin to think in a certain way.

This in turn helps to create social proof that the concepts are working, which reinforces your belief.

When you revisit the concepts presented here with some regularity, improving your thoughts each time, you will begin to notice dramatic shifts. We know we have.

Observations of Certain Ways

More from Sandi: I have found that the more I recognize my certain way, the more I recognize the certain way of others.

I am always looking for inspiring people that have a certain way in something they are doing. I am in awe of musicians, performers, and every day people who have a certain way that comes through in everything that they do. It is as if they can convince you of something by simply being and doing—it is hard to describe a certain way—the closest that I can come is that it is when you can feel someone's almost effortless intensity.

I like to surround myself with people who have a desire to grow. I look for inspiration from people who make something look effortless. I grow my thoughts and expand my horizons by looking to people who are living in a different paradigm.

I surround myself with people with big ideas, happy people, and people who don't follow the norm.

If you begin to do this, every once in a while, you notice someone and they will seem to have a different outlook of life about them. Pay attention.

Who you are and what you do are different, and so much can be gleaned from observing this in the people that you meet. Except for engineers, engineers are normally an engineer.

"There is no such thing as the lack of opportunities for the man who is living the advancing life and who has an advancing mind." —Wallace Wattles

The Certain Way Described As a Wave

By Monica Tombers

"As we were discussing "Our Certain Way" at our last marketing club meeting, an image formed in my head.

Picture a beautiful pond that is so calm that there is not a ripple to be seen.

If I pick a certain spot on that pond to focus my attention, I can create a lovely consistent pattern. As I let a drop fall on my target, concentric wave circles are formed and spread out until their energy is dispersed. Each following drop grows my circle of influence on the water.

If I take my focus off that certain spot and allow my drop to fall outside of the target, the concentric pattern will be interrupted and lose its momentum and influence.

The more and longer I do this, the more chaotic the waves will be and the less effective each drop will be.

I can change my focus from one spot to another and there will always be a period of chaos until the old energy has dissipated. Yet nothing will give me the power of a consistent pattern more than keeping my focus... on my certain wave."

Why Change?

Why is it important to evolve a company if it works? Why not stay the same?

Staying the same is a short term view. Everything changes. You need to continually innovate or you'll look around one day and the world will have changed and you will be left wondering what happened.

We can easily look at examples of companies who have been old school in their thinking and have been reluctant to change. Ready-Mix concrete companies are an example of this in the pool industry. We are sure you can think of some more on your own.

Why use our Organic Marketing™ Process?

Marketing has changed dramatically with the changes in technology and the social tools that we now have access to.

With the dawn of the social network online, how we engage, interact, and build our relationships has undergone a profound and irreversible shift.

How does a business owner or professional begin to play in the new social sandbox?

You can follow our process to help you do just that; a simple to use and incredibly powerful tool for defining your marketing goals, creating an authentic and energetic online presence, and managing your interactions. We call it *Organic Marketing™*.

You start with the common Tic-Tac-Toe[2] concept for the layout and use each square to flesh out your online signature, your connections, your social sphere, your customers, and six other critical elements that make up your overall marketing strategy.

By methodically working on each square, you become comfortable in playing the game; making those "three across" winning connections and using social media as a powerful business tool.

---

[2] Fun Fact according Wikipedia to An early variant of Tic-Tac-Toe was played in the Roman Empire, around the first century BC.

There is no doubt about this: You need to be present socially online. Show up with authenticity, with consistency, and with a clear understanding of how to connect your efforts. When you put the right pieces in place to leverage your social sphere, your business will grow organically and you will love the results!

The Law of Effortless Allowance

Al is the "philosophy guy" and has coined a term we embrace called "The Law of Effortless Allowance."

When an individual or a company begins to plan a new strategy there is the tendency to set a course, and hold so tightly to that course that it may become almost too rigid.

Instead, when planning our future we need to think through the process of what it is we want. We should go through the mental exercises to get us ready and prepared for what is to come, and then we need to let it go.

If you hold a thought in your mind, and if you think about it over and over to discover all that there is that you need to know and plan about it, you may become too wrapped up in the planning and the orchestration that it stifles the process.

For example, consider a coach and team. They will practice, practice, and practice. They will go over drills to learn the moves and the plays. They will plan routes and how the team will perform on game day. Once game day happens, sometimes the team gets in their own way and begins to perform more poorly than they expected. Mistakes may happen when they start to try too hard, trying to overcome their opponents.

This is often because the players, and sometimes the coach, try to orchestrate the game and their movements, instead of allowing. When faced with the reality of the game, sometimes they can mentally get caught up and forget to allow. If they can let go and effortlessly allow the game to unfold, trust in the coach, trust in the team, and trust that they already have the strategy and all the skills they need in place, they can proceed with well practiced, comfortable actions.

It is the same in business. All things that are practiced and thought about can become easy.

It is the same in marketing. If you go through this process in the book, and think about it in each section, you will put into place all of the thoughts and strategies you will need to be successful.

The magic will then be in letting go.

In the Buddhist belief, it's known as stepping into the river right where you are.

In our culture, we are programmed to think that things take work, they take struggles. We are encouraged to swim against the current, and just swim faster and harder to overcome it.

The Buddhist belief is much simpler. Step into the river and allow it to take you in the natural path where the water is going to flow.

We apply this concept to marketing and to life, and refer to it as the "Law of Effortless Allowance."

We have heard the old adage many, many times, that life is not the destination, it is the journey.

Likewise, there is no destination in business; it is the journey of your Certain Way that will bring you everything you set out to achieve.

Work on your Certain Way, and go through the exercises we introduce in this book. Then, let go and effortlessly allow it to unfold. You will enjoy the process, and be encouraged by the results.

This is the secret to the "Law of Effortless Allowance." We put it into practice when we created the InSights Community, we put it into practice when we reinvented the pool company by working on Our Certain Way, and we live by it to this day.

"Everything that touches your life is an opportunity if you discover its proper use."
—Wallace Wattles

When in Doubt, Write a Book

We have followed Seth Godin, his books and his blog for years. When Seth defines a new concept, he writes a book about it. We thought we'd do the same with Organic Marketing™ and his inspiration is the reason you are reading this book right now.

Everything we do to market our company we first began to explore during our entrepreneur support center days at the InSights Community.

We started to talk about concepts of organic growth and we found it covered much more than just one type of improvement.

It wasn't just about marketing; it was about making ourselves and our companies stronger. This concept that worked for one company was also effective to implement, perhaps with a twist, in another company.

We've grown organically, much the same way social media does when it works.

We've come to learn that leadership is needed to create a community of enthusiasm, of spontaneity, of people who are willing to jump in with both feet.

The world of social media mirrors a business environment; you have to be willing to jump in, and you have to expect the unexpected. The physical part of things—the furniture, the arrangement of the space, the décor, the site, the people, and the function of your favorite social media site is continually changing, so don't get complacent and don't get too comfortable. The people, the leaders, the followers and the relationships you build with them, are your foundation for a great platform.

Social media requires people to become great storytellers, to be creative, and to have a little bit of fun.

Social Media is blending the best of both worlds—our personal interactions and our business lives—in an entirely new way.

The secret to success in social media is in finding the balance. Take our InSights entrepreneur Community for example: some of our best meetings have included games of Duck-Duck-Goose or Twister, played on the floor by business people ranging in age from 20 to 70.

The same holds true for social media interaction. When business is truly fun and engaging, business grows and changes as the people behind the business get out of their ruts and expand their possibilities.

Social media allows us to, think bigger and find resources at our fingertips. We have an incredible opportunity to surround ourselves with people who are positive, forward-thinking and supportive, and who share our belief that anything is possible.

This is the spirit of the new media. Embrace it!

Live in the Land of "What If?"

Social media is about stories and connecting people. it makes sense to start with a discussion of "What if?"

The question that started our journey with the InSights Community was "What if?" "What if we existed to help people, be better, do better, and explore big ideas?" That, my friend, is also the key to social media.

If you enter the social media conversation asking how you can help, you're in the greatest power position you can imagine.

When you care about what people are doing, you can be anywhere in the world, and people will pay attention to what you have to say. Stopping in to visit you online could be just the thing that they needed to feel good, get inspired, learn something, or create a new way of thinking. Be open to the possibilities that new media opens up for you. Use new media to connect with people and become part of a community that you want to grow with. You will become more like the people you associate with, so be sure to associate with good people.

As Charlie Tremendous Jones, in his book *Life is Tremendous* says, "You will be exactly who you are in five years with the exception of the people you associate with and the books that you read."

Great connections will help you evolve into a new version of yourself. You can take thought and inspiration from those around you. Be aware of this so you can surround yourself with the right people to help you improve.

Read good books, read good blogs, share your message, surround yourself with good people, and think bigger than you could possibly ever have imagined. The books you read evolve your mind. What you read today will have an impact on what you are doing tomorrow. You can look at someone else and say "I can do that."

Who is on your list of people that have great stories and can help you think bigger?

The Dynamic of an Effective Partnership

We have an added bonus of a mastermind duo within our Al and Sandi mindshare. We challenge each other every day, all the time to never stay the same. We continually go all in, all the time on our endeavors. We are visionary, eccentric, love practical oddities, visual, old fashioned, and trendy all at the same time. One of the best alliances you can find for yourself during this process is a mastermind partner to go through this exploration with. Someone who is where you are, and able to see things from a new perspective, and that you can bounce ideas back and forth with will be valuable on this journey.

A Note about Marketing and Advertising

The words marketing and advertising are often used interchangeably. We would like to make a distinction. Marketing is the process of sharing a message with people; the purpose of that message is to shorten the sales cycle.

Advertising is placing a specific message in front of someone to get them to purchase a particular product or service. Advertising is often less personal in scope, versus marketing which is based on a more personal, relationship building concept.

An advertising campaign is often a single part of a larger marketing strategy. When we talk about advertising within Organic Marketing ™, the actual advertisement may be a piece of paper, a page on a website, a postcard, or even a business card that is used to encourage someone to do something.

Advertising is a thing, a tool.

Marketing is a whole plan.

A good marketing strategy creates awareness within people about a product or service, influences their desire, and results in an inspired action. A good marketing strategy can influence the mind of the prospect, in a subtly motivating way.

The Marketing Bubble

To help conceptualize marketing, let's discuss the concept of the marketing bubble as explained by Al.

Close your eyes and picture your ideal client in your mind.

Next, picture a giant bubble around your client. This bubble isolates your client from the more than 50,000 marketing messages we are exposed to each day. All these messages bombard your prospect every day and most just bounce off their bubble. Your greatest challenge is to get your message inside of their bubble. You want to be noticed by your ideal target client.

Rather than pierce the bubble by force (popping), good marketing softens the edge of the bubble. By getting your message in front of your client as often as possible, perhaps by pulling up alongside the bubble unobtrusively, or being in the periphery, the person inside their bubble might begin to take notice. Hopefully they get closer to the edge of the bubble to peek outside.

Maybe you get them so curious that they will take their bubble even closer to your bubble. (Think bumper-bubbles that is pretty cool!)

The more curious your prospect becomes, the more of your message you can share. Craft your message in a way that helps them identify their desire to hear more and see for themselves what it is that you offer.

Once you have a prospect (in their own bubble) paying attention, the marketing and subsequent advertising that you put out will more likely result in an action; it could be a purchase, a mental book mark for a later purchase, or sharing your message with people in their sphere of influence. In the world of social media, the goal is the share. You really, really want people to be sharing your messages and stories with their own social networks.

An effective marketing campaign will have everyone who is separated from you (by their own bubble) vying for position, trying to get a glimpse of what you have going on.

As a result, instead of selling anything to them, they are selling themselves to you by listening to your story and seeing themselves using your product or service.

If advertising is targeted towards the eventual sale of a product, think of your marketing as creating the awareness that you exist, whether you are in a bubble or not.

Effective marketing will remove the need for the "hard sell."

Organic Marketing™ Inspiration

One of the important aspects of the InSights Community, from the beginning, was the concept of "Masterminding." Gathering a group of like-minded, enthusiastic and motivated business owners together on a regular basis, to share, brainstorm and support each other. This has been a core feature of our philosophy.

It was during one such Mastermind Meeting that the Organic Marketing™ concept crystallized out of thin air. As it happens sometimes in a Mastermind meeting, the mind wanders and is able to tap into pure inspired thought.

Sandi was in the zone, downloading some inspired ideas directly from the business cosmos.

She put her pen to the journal, the one she carries into each meeting, and began drawing. Then she quietly rose, went to the front of the room, drew her vision on the whiteboard, and sat back down.

Organic Marketing
TIC - TAC - TOE

	Business	Personal	Universe
Business	Connections	Social Networks	Target Audience
Personal	Energy Signature	you	The Stuff
Universe	TLC Think Like your Customer	Alliances	Home

Of course, everyone in the room wanted to know more. The initial explanation took no more than a few minutes.

There was a moment of stunned silence, and then a chorus of "Brilliant!" Organic Marketing™ and the Marketing Tic-Tac-Toe™ concept was born.

Marketing—Tic-Tac-Toe™ Style

The concept looks deceptively simple. It lives in a tic-tac-toe board, with each of the nine squares representing a part of you and/or your business.

So what's the secret that is locked in the layout of the Marketing Tic-Tac-Toe™ board?

Simply put, Tic-Tac-Toe™ breaks down your marketing efforts into three categories:

➢ Personal
➢ Business
➢ Universe

These define the squares in relationship to each other, and become the axis for navigating the squares.

By placing the axis on the board, and discovering the corresponding squares, you are able to create a visual short-hand to help you understand how to reach new audiences, build new relationships and grow your business, within an easy framework.

We are often asked how social media is so different from traditional media. Here's the secret; it's not that different.

Social media is not about using a new media in an old way. It's about using the media available today to communicate with people *in the way they choose.* Understanding this makes all the difference in the world.

Success in social media is first about relationship building, which is and always has been at the heart of effective marketing.

Navigating the Tic-Tac-Toe Board

Now that you have a better understanding of what marketing is all about, let's see how this applies to the Organic Marketing™ Tic-Tac-Toe concept. By using this strategic tool, you gain a clearer perspective of your marketing activities and understand why you are doing them.

Now let's take a closer look at the board that will be used as the basis for all of your Organic Marketing™ efforts moving forward. As you become familiar with this process, you will also begin to see a variety of other applications. We'll keep sharing examples of these applications along the way.

Each square on the Organic Marketing™ Tic-Tac-Toe board is independent, and at the same time, they are all connected.

We lay out the board starting with the axis on top and down the side: (in left to right and top to bottom order). Across the top is business, personal, universe, and down the side are business, personal, and universe.

When we define this board, business activities are just that. Personal, are your activities with closer relationships. The Universe represents things that you just do for the sake of putting positive energy out there, and are not worried about when things will come back your way. It is marketing to the world, and being open to people finding you as a result of your awesome Organic Marketing™ Strategies.

Organic Marketing
TIC - TAC - TOE

	Business	Personal	Universe
Business	Connections	Social Networks	TPrager Target Audience
Personal	Energy Signature	you	TH Stuff
Universe	TLC Think Like your Customer	Alliances	Home

You will notice that the axis puts the squares in specific relation to each other. The Energy Signature square, for example, matches the Personal/Business Axis. This is the square where you develop your "persona," so people get a warm and friendly, personal, introduction to your brand and your business.

Moving from left to right, and starting at the top, the squares contain the following concepts:

> ➤ Line 1:

>> ✓ Connections
>> ✓ Social Networks
>> ✓ Your Target Audience

> ➤ Line 2:

>> ✓ Energy Signature
>> ✓ YOU
>> ✓ The "Stuff"

> ➤ Line 3:

>> ✓ TLC—"Think Like your Customer"
>> ✓ Strategic Alliances
>> ✓ Your Online House

Just as in playing a real Tic-Tac-Toe game, there is an order to the squares and a strategy to be used to create a winning combination.

Navigating Organic Marketing™ the 1st Time

Using the Organic Marketing™ Tic-Tac-Toe board is a bit like a choose-your-own-adventure novel. You can jump in at any square you'd like.

The first time around the board, however, or anytime you are using this model to launch a new discussion, go through the squares in this order:

1) You {Middle Square}
2) Target {Top, Right}
3) Think Like a Customer {Bottom, Left}
4) Energy Signature {Middle, Left}
5) Connections {Top, Left}
6) Social Networks {Top, Middle}
7) The Stuff {Middle, Right}
8) Alliances {Bottom, Middle}
9) Home: your Website {Bottom, Right}

Not that you've got the basics covered, we will get started with You, the {Middle Square} of the board.

YOU

{Middle Square}

Work becomes play when we are truly passionate about what we do.

Al explains: We've all heard the old cliché saying that if you love what you do, you'll never work another day in your life. Still, a lot of us struggle with this idea. I know I used to. I was conditioned to view work as something necessary, not something to truly enjoy.

Until I discovered one simple truth: happiness is a choice. I can choose to be happy in each situation, or I can choose not to be. I can choose to be excited about moving forward or choose to remain stuck right where I am.

For me, happiness and passion for what I am doing go hand in hand. I've consciously made the decision that I'm going to love what I do, and I'm only going to take on the work that I love. If it doesn't excite me, if I think it's going to be a drag, I turn down the job.

What about you? What kind of work makes you excited? What kind of jobs should you walk away from? As you think about the first square on the grid, keep an ear open to hear your truths. It's where it all starts.

Know your Why!

If you have ever picked up the book *Start With Why*[3] by Simon Sinek[i], or listened to the TED talk of the same name, you know how important it is to Start with your Why.

Knowing why you do what you do helps to become the basis to frame your entire message about your life's work, or at least your present moment work. This helps to frame all of your future marketing as well.

---

[3] If you have access to the internet and have not yet watched Simon Sinek's TED Talk (available on YouTube), please take a few moments to do that now, we'll wait...

When you know your way, you can move forward with a focused plan for the future. When all members of an organization can clearly understand and communicate the Why of the company, and how their personal Why fits into it, they can move forward with purpose.

When all the members of an organization fully know and can articulate their why, the individuals and the company will exude their Certain Way. This is a signal of security that customers will be able to recognize, and make the decisions to work with your organization so much easier!

Customers look for security when choosing a company to do business with. They want reassurance in knowing their product or service needs will be handled well. Establishing a personal and company culture can help you create this essence of securing what your audience is looking for.

Social media started out as the new social trend that, we have found is here to stay. It has fundamentally shifted our style of communication. What started out as a way to communicate with friends and family quickly became a way to reach prospects and customers. We have been able to share stories and have more interaction than marketers have before.

While we (individuals or companies) are having conversations online, social media is a natural outlet for people who know us and like us to talk about us. If they like what they see, they will interact with us, and with their connections by spreading the message about us via social sharing. This can include who we are, what we do, and how they have done business with us.

Unlike traditional methods of businesses talking *at* people, social media is a way for businesses to talk **with** people and engage in conversations.

Ask yourself this question: Does it have more of an impact on you if your best friend recommends a product or service or if the sales person at the store tells you about something that you should buy?

Most of the time, we tend to make decisions based on the recommendation of our friends and family over that of a salesperson. There are times, of course, when the expertise of a salesperson is needed to close the deal; but to get your foot in the door, to get inside the bubble, and to get you into the position to buy, the recommendations of the people who you know, love, and trust have weight.

Social media provides an opportunity to engage with a wide audience, adding the personal referral and recommendation as a new, natural social conversation.

This new engagement is a departure from the traditional "interruption marketing" that, by definition, interrupts what we are doing, watching, or listening to. Interruption marketing has given way to what Seth Godin calls "permission marketing[ii]," in which people choose to participate in groups, discussions, forums, and other online conversations. They are there by choice, and so have fewer barriers to the messages they are exposed to.

Define a Personal Mission/Vision

When you *Start with Why*, you can move from your overall guiding Why into a personal mission and vision for yourself, or your organization.

All too often we find that during a planning session a company will jump right into defining a mission statement. Without starting with why the mission ends up representing a whole lot of *what* a company does, not *why* they do it. This is a huge distinction. Your Why needs to translate into your mission for it to be the most beneficial.

The development and understanding of your mission is an important component of the center square. We typically think in terms of mission statements for business, but it's just as important, maybe even more so, to have a clear personal mission and vision for your life.

A mission statement for a business typically addresses what an organization is all about. It answers the questions: *What do you do? For whom do you do it? What is the benefit?* Think about these for you personally as well, and perhaps as it applies to your place in an organization or as a solo-preneur.

You define your mission statement, but just as importantly, your mission statement helps to define you. The mission statement identifies your core values, the reasons you do what you do, and it identifies your intentions. A solid mission clarifies what you bring to the organization, or to the world, and identifies **why** it is important to you.

As an example, when we began to frame the Mission Statement for Ask the Pool Guy, we started with our Why. We wanted to change the world as a result of being active in the pool industry.

As we began looking toward the future for our "Ask the Pool Guy" brand, we summed up our mission with these words:

Happy Pools. Happy Customers. Happy Pool Guy.

This became the basis for all of our business decisions, customer service policies, and marketing efforts. We discovered if the pools we serviced could be happy, then our customers would be happy, and our team (and Pool Guy) could be happy as well.

When we put these together, our personal mission and our business mission, we create a clear, defined path to follow. This becomes our guide for all of our marketing efforts (and business decisions) and helps us establish where we will make a difference in the world.

Through the Organic Marketing™ strategies, in the subsequent squares, you are going to think through this process and be able to develop a message to share your unique abilities and talents with the world, and learn from other people who share theirs.

Use all of these elements to enhance your message. There is not one component of this process that can stand alone. They all work together to create an awesome blueprint and the subsequent building blocks for a truly awesome presence and awareness in the world.

You have all the tools at your fingertips to make sure that you have the highest probability of success.

If you have a team working with you, make sure you include input and work on this together as you build your vision for the future.

It is fun to include the team when developing all of the pieces. If you have ten people, you have ten personalities; you have ten ways of thinking, and ten different types of motivation to consider, as well as ten ways to tell stories and ten "characters" to include as you share your story with the world.

Taking a personality assessment at this point would be extremely helpful. Consider the popular DiSC or Personality Plus[4] tests as a resource and have a discussion of the results guided by someone who can lend some insight into what the results mean for your organization.

As we move into the next squares in the process of developing and navigating the board,

---

[4] See the End Notes for where to find this quick and simple test, as well as descriptions to help your team understand each other better.

we will utilize the personality types in aiding all of our efforts. Understanding the four main types of personalities is going to help you understand yourself, your team, and ultimately how to understand and interact with your target audience.

If we had to choose a square as the most important to this entire process, it would be the center square. Spend plenty of time on this center square of YOU, and revisit it often as you develop the rest of your tic-tac-toe board. It is the most important square to figure out, as it becomes the foundation around which all of your decisions will be made.

The core of Organic Marketing™ is YOU, and is the most important element on the board. Make sure that you have clarity in this square. Without that, no matter how much you try, your message will be missing a critical piece.

Plogos and Physiognomy

A "plogo" is a concept we developed at the InSights Community (with a little help from our friend @tjlist[5]) during one of our Social Media training sessions. We have coached business owners, entrepreneurs, and teams for years that, to be visible in social media and form solid relationships with people, they need to have their photo on all of their profiles. Many of our clients raised the legitimate concern that they also need to co-brand and represent their company online. Enter the "plogo," a photo and logo used in combination to represent both the company, and the individual person simultaneously.

---

[5] Look him up on Twitter, he is an Automotive Engineer by day and a WordPress Geek by Night (and an all around fun guy).

Just imagine how effective this is for teams of people. Using the company logo, combined with an individual photo, each person has their individual plogo they can share on Twitter, Facebook, and in their email signature.

This combines the relationship-building power of a each person with the brand recognition of the company and creates a unique voice for the brand and that of each individual. This works for a solo-preneur as well, it helps to showcase you and the work you do branded together very effectively.

An Entrepreneur can use this to their benefit when they are communicating online. Take for example an insurance agent who represents ABC Company. When they consistently include their name as the primary brand on social media, with the undercurrent of their current company, people become used to doing business with them.

If something, such as a corporate relationship, ever changes for them in the future, it is easier to communicate with their clients and friends about the change. When a relationship is developed with a person, it can supersede a brand. Independent insurance agents want to offer you the best choice for your circumstances; they build their brand on their personal dedication to obtain the best deal for you.

We are Visual Connectors

As humans we tend to be visual connectors. We are drawn to faces. One of the first things we notice about someone is their face and their facial expression. Are they happy, sad, in shock? Can we tell what mood they are in by what their face is telling us?

Every company has a "face." For us it is a cartoon—*Ask the Pool Guy*. We even use it to distinguish between four company offerings.

The image you choose to feature as the face of your company, or on your social media profiles, can also be a normal professional picture of the boss, the whole team, or just one outstanding individual.

The most important part is that you make sure it is a photo that is very representative of the people of your company or organization. It is the people that will set you apart.

We see many companies that are missing the personal aspect in their online interactions. It has gotten better since companies first started using social media, though we still notice who the new adopters are. Remember at its core social media is about personal interaction. Having a recognizable picture or logo will really improve your chances of building the connection with your potential customers.

There may be some cases where it is more important that the company take center stage, with the person who is servicing them in a supporting role. With *Ask the Pool Guy*, for example, our service team members introduce themselves with "Ask the Pool Guy, my name is Mark." This way, our customers know that any member of our team with *Ask the Pool Guy* will give them great service, and they don't have to depend on a relationship with just one person to meet their needs. In their interaction they are having with our team member, they will have very personalized one-on-one service.

Service Team Leader
Mark Curtis

Ask the
POOLGUY

This is the front of Mark's business card. Now there is a face with friendliness and determination to take care of your pool needs.

History of Communication

The history of human communication includes both words and visual cues. Before electronic communication became the norm, we learned as much with our eyes as we did with our ears.

With social media, where we do not have the visual cue of the actual person in front of us, the importance of social interaction and human connection through pictures is even greater. Since marketing is about creating relationships, using a photo with a logo lets you accomplish the best of both worlds.

Physiognomy: Face Reading

As social creatures, humans are innately drawn to other human faces. Physiognomy is the study of the human face, and specifically the study of how facial features represent our thought processes.

Physiognomy[6] (from the Gk. physis meaning "nature" and gnomon meaning "judge" or "interpreter") is the assessment of a person's character or personality from his or her outer appearance, especially the face.

As we go through life, the process of how we think literally becomes etched on our faces. The human brain inherently picks up on subtle cues

---

[6] *https://en.wikipedia.org/wiki/**Physiognomy***

on faces, and helps us understand each other from a visual level. The attributes on our face help others gain a better understanding of us. Physiognomy is innately understood by the brain, whether we are conscious of it or not[7].

The Importance of Understanding Face Reading

In the new economy and its dependence on online connections for relationship building, we must stretch the boundaries of our communication and think of new ways to truly create a human connection. The easiest way is to use our most human asset—our own face.

Facial recognition starts building neuro-pathways in our brain and creates a sense of comfort. We form a sense of knowing and common ground when we meet someone in person after seeing their picture online. The relationship builds even if we never meet in person, as so many of our relationships will exist only through our interaction online.

Marketing is about finding common ground and then building on that relationship. When someone shares our social space, and we have glimpsed their life through pictures and videos, we feel a sense of connection. When a photo is

---

[7] You already know more about face reading than you thought you did. Congratulations!

included, our brains engage at a higher capacity and we have a sense of greater connection. Being the social creatures that we are, once we've seen someone's face, we feel that we know them on a personal level.

Now would be a great way to look at the images you are using online for your social profiles. Make sure you are using happy, smiling images. It is also a great time to get some new ones processed, and to spend some time doing a little research in understanding physiognomy (the art of face reading[8]) even more.

Look at your Business as a Work of Art

Now that we've talked about the art of face reading, let's move into another area where art can help us during our marketing and storytelling. Approach your business as an artist would, and see and describe it as a work of art.

All too often a business is treated as just something someone does. The business and profession become one. If you take a moment to think about your business as a work of art, you can begin to develop a whole new appreciation for it, and the messages you need to share begin to develop themselves.

---

[8] Look for some fun videos from Al and Sandi that will help you learn to enhance your face reading talents.

One small business owner, who was at the cusp of launching her business, was holding back out of fear of what the business would become.

As she took another approach and determined her business could be her work of art, she began to see its potential. Instead of her business just existing as others wanted it to, she could mold and shape every aspect of the customer's engagement with her services.

It created a freeing feeling for her to approach not only her service offering, but also her business as its own piece of art for her to mold and shape as she wanted it to be.

@RitaLongArt paints on Lake Shannon

When you frame your business as a piece of art and move into the marketing stages, it will allow you to ask and answer these questions.

- ✓ What do you see in the business?
- ✓ How does it make you feel?

- ✓ What makes up the business, in the foreground? How about in the background, that the customer may not see?
- ✓ How do people see your business?
- ✓ How does your business make them feel?
- ✓ Are there other perspectives or vantage points you are missing because you are only looking at one side of things?
- ✓ When you treat your business as a piece of art you are also more open to change things, improve upon them, and "paint over," in effect, things that become old or outdated.

There may be swirls of improvement, splashes of success and errors. All of this can be molded and changed. The best thing about marketing in today's social spheres is that your message can be changed quickly and you can release updates as frequently as you like.

@allancurtis paints @insightsgroup

With your message shaped and continually evolving about your work of art, you can flow through changes and growth like a river, full of turbulent rapids, or you can find serene coves and coast along in one particular message for a while. Enjoy the entire realm of whimsical sunsets, great mountains, and the roaring rivers as you share your stories.

Work of Art Exercise

Thinking of your business as a work of art; now is a great time to jump into this exercise.

Begin by answering these questions for yourself:

- ✓ Is your business maturing or standing still?
- ✓ How much do you feel your business is worth? Is it becoming more valuable (appreciating) over time? If not, what should you begin to do to improve things?
- ✓ Is the business making you feel fulfilled? If it is not, what would make it more fulfilling?
- ✓ Does your business energize you every day? If not, what could you do to make it more exciting and energizing, for both yourself, and your customers?
- ✓ From the client perspective, are they a "collector" who is excited every time you have an update, or has your work become stale and predictable?
- ✓ What type of journey would you like to take your customers on next?
- ✓ Finally, place yourself in the artwork. How do you feel as an individual within the piece? Do you feel integrated and connected with the business? Why or why not?

We encourage you to write down or journal the answers to these questions. As silly as you may feel at first, we promise you'll come to discover a whole new awareness about yourself and your business by doing this activity.

Confidence in YOU and Confidence in your Why

Confidence is essential. When you feel you are on top of the world, or on top of your game, you will master anything that you decide to do. This includes the marketing and growth for yourself and your business.

Here is a story that Sandi has enjoyed telling about when she was awed by the confidence of her son's soccer team a number of years ago.

Sandi's son played indoor soccer and was on a team that was made up of 8 year olds through 12 year olds, playing an age level up in the 11- and 12-year-old age group. They were put together as a skilled, competitive team and in spite of the variety of ages of the players they were a winning team.

Toward the end of the season, when the score of the game was no longer a factor, the coach decided that he would like to challenge these boys; he would help them bring up their skill level. Instead of putting all of them out on the field, he pulled two off, so they were playing the first half of the soccer game two men down.

The coach knew that the boys had all the skills and abilities they would need. He wanted to make the game a bit more challenging by making them work a little bit harder. As we came to find out, the boys weren't as confident as they had been when they had all their men on the field. They started making small mistakes. They were not working together as a team, and for the first time all season, the score was reversed. They didn't score a goal the entire first half and the other team scored on them repeatedly.

From the sidelines, the parents could see what was happening, and the coach could see it too. He wanted to help the boys find that inner confidence and figure out what they needed to do to be successful.

At halftime, the coach had a talk with the boys. He decided to put the last two men back on the field. Instantly, the confidence level changed. They started scoring goals—five in a row without even thinking about it. The only thing that had changed was their perspective. Their skill level had not improved. Their tactics and abilities had not improved. It was the simple factor of their perception in their confidence that made the difference.

How confident are you in your business? Do you let outside influences change your perspective? Do you look at the competition and see somebody else that is bigger, that has more tools or more abilities, and let that affect you?

Let the lessons of the soccer game be a lesson to you as well. You have all the tools and abilities that you could possibly need. You simply need to focus on the confidence that you have within, just like the boys on the soccer field.

Don't stop to think that the odds are against you. Dig a little deeper and focus your energy so you are more effective. You have what it takes to be successful; you simply need to recognize that.

Defining Your Certain Way

The Center Square of You should take the most time to contemplate. It will be a work in progress as you grow and change. Take the time to set a clear "North" for yourself as you begin this process. As we move through the other squares, be sure to revisit this as you discover more about yourself and gain even more clarity as you navigate the Organic Marketing™ Tic-Tac-Toe Board.

Your Target Audience

{Top, Right}

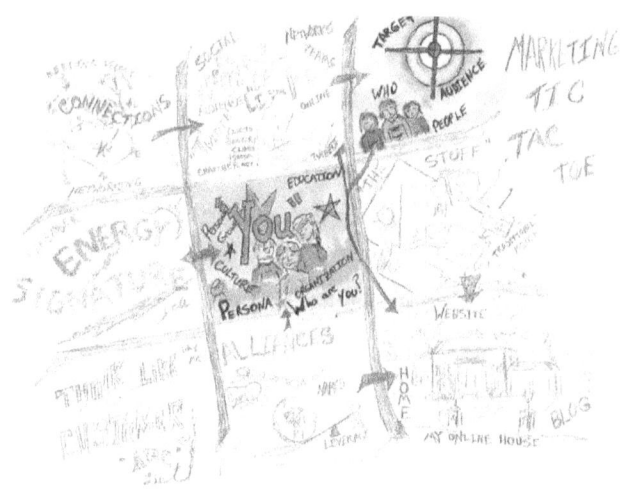

How to find the right customer with the right attitude and the right energy

The customer is always right; except when they are wrong[9].

---

[9] And, especially when they are wrong for you.

This is a truth we've discovered in this business. By wrong we don't mean "mistaken" or "incorrect." A customer can be completely justified in what they want …and still be entirely wrong for you.

In this new connection economy *who* you choose to do business with is just as important as *what* you choose to do. Not everyone should be your customer; yet learning to turn down potential business can be terrifying and seem counter-intuitive.

For us, this paradigm shift began at the end of a particularly challenging project. The homeowner was beyond thrilled with the results of our planning and hard labor. As he happily wrote the final check, he turned to Al and said, "You know, you could have charged me 50% more for this project and I would have paid it, no question."

This left Al stunned. While he drove home that day, he began contemplating how he had been undervaluing his work, and charging what the average pool owner would have wanted to pay. Clearly he was worth more than he thought, and having it pointed out by one of our customers was a light bulb moment.

Our ideal customer, we realized, would be the home owner who wants something out of the ordinary, something epic even, and is willing to give us the artistic leeway (and the budget!) to create that vision.

Creating a business that truly feeds your soul begins with knowing your true value in the marketplace and honoring that value by only working with the customers that "get it."

Target within Your Universe

In the overall plan of Organic Marketing™ Tic-Tac-Toe, it's important to define a target within your universe. You need to define your target customer, their personality, and discover where to find them.

Taking the time to define your target—the person who is ultimately going to buy your product or service—is the best way to determine which marketing decisions to make.

When you create your marketing plan with this in mind, you can develop each future square directly for the benefit of reaching your end consumer. This serves you in a few different ways:

1) Your message will be specific and relevant, so the person who receives that message understands what you do, and what they need to do to work with you.

2) Your marketing messages will build bridges. Some of the people who intercept your message are going to be connections or bridges to your final customer. They need to know, by looking at that marketing piece, who to direct it to. They should be able to see it and recognize who would be a perfect connection for you.

3) Well focused messages will help your ultimate customer understand that they need YOU. If you have targeted properly, they will

immediately feel the connection with you. They will choose themselves as your customer and will understand who you are, what you do, why it is important to do business with you, and how to hire you.

Define Your Target Customer?

To define your target audience let's look at these questions regarding your target clients:

1) Who are your existing best and favorite customers? Would you like more of them? (If this answer is not clear, please take the time to go back to the middle square to re-evaluate your Why, and develop some thoughts on who you would like to work with.)

If you are just launching a business, consult your Why and determine who you will best serve in your new venture. Get specific about the types of services they will need, and how your *why* will match up with what they are looking for.

2) Next, determine some of the characteristics of your target customer, so you can begin to custom build your message for them as your audience.

- ✓ Who do you want to reach?
- ✓ What are their demographics?
- ✓ Are they geographically located in one area?
- ✓ Is your business constrained to a geographic location or is it universal?

- ✓ Are there commonalities that your target audience possesses?
- ✓ Income levels?
- ✓ Job titles?
- ✓ Ways of making decisions?
- ✓ Certain Values?
- ✓ Hobbies?
- ✓ Associations?
- ✓ Does your product or service appeal most to men or women?
- ✓ Who tends to buy your product the most?
- ✓ Next, consider the age demographic. What age range most often buys from you?

When you've identified even these simple trends, you can see how you can begin to make choices for your outgoing messages based on this.

For example, if you sell to customers aged 75 years old and older, social media probably isn't the best place to focus.

On the other hand, if your product is marketed to people between the ages of 20 to 50 years old, social media has a lot of potential for you. You can then narrow the segment even more. Define the age range even more. Are they 35 to 50 years old? Are they 30 to 40 years old?

What are some common characteristics of your client mix?

The answers to these questions will help you identify exactly who you are speaking to. Do it on paper. This is important, and you will revisit refining your target audience along your journey discovering the rest of your tic-tac-toe board.

If you are not clear on this, you are not alone. We often sit down with clients to talk about marketing strategy and quickly realize that they have no idea who they are really marketing to.

There aren't many businesses that can truly market to everyone.

Your business has a target audience. It has a specific sweet spot where your message and your *why* will resonate and people will find out and know they have to hire you. That audience may be niche market or it may be a larger segment of the population.

You must become very clear about who your target really is. In this way, you increase your odds of success and you can laser focus your marketing efforts and your message. You will also know clearly when they contact you if they meet your target audience criteria.

Determining Personality Types

This is based largely on the classic personality theory based on the work of Hippocrates of Kos[10] (460-370 BC). You can find plenty of information online by searching for "Hippocratic personality types." There are many resources available to study the four basic

---

[10] Greek physician of the Age of Pericles (Classical Greece), and is considered one of the most outstanding figures in the history of medicine

personality types[11] and apply the learning to your life. The four basic personality types that we will discuss are: the Driver, the Detail Person, the Fun Lover, and the Laid Back relaxed type.

The Choleric (Driver) wants information quickly, concisely, in bullet points; you must make it easy for them to find the information they need, because they are on the move. You need to be aggressive and sharp to capture this buyer.

The Melancholy (Detail Person) wants to absorb all of the criteria and all of the information before they make decisions, so you must cater to them differently. You must have all the information they may need, and then some, available to them.

The Sanguine (Fun Lover) just wants to have a good time, regardless of what they are doing. Their whole purpose in life, everything they are about, is having fun. If they are not having fun, they are miserable, so you'll want to target part of your social media strategy toward these types of people, taking into account how would they interact and how would you interact with them.

The Phlegmatic (Laid Back & Loyal) type represents almost 40% of the population. These

---

[11] We suggest *Personality Plus* by Florence Littauer (1992). Revel, as an additional read in the study of personality types.

folks are slow to convert, so you must be available to them in many ways, times, and places so that when they are finally ready, you are there in front of them.

You will want to do a basic personality test[12] to determine your personality baseline, and find additional resources to learn how to relate and communicate best with all personality types[13]. Then you can compare and contrast to your target audience and work on communication.

Consider the personality types outlined here as you define your target audience. Each type of personality needs to see messages and be communicated with in their own unique way. When you can segment your messages moving forward to address each of the members of your audience, you'll be able to deliver compelling content to each person, in their own preferred style.

Defining Your Certain Way

Becoming clear about your Target Audience is key in this square. As you recognize your best

---

[12] Take the test in the book Personality Plus as the quickest way to gain some knowledge about yourself and your audience.

[13] Sandi has a great discussion of personality on the website www.askthepoolguy.com/marketing.

clients, this square will become even easier to define. We will continue to revisit personality types as we navigate the Organic Marketing™ Tic-Tac-Toe board, so keep your notes handy!

TLC—Think Like your Customer

{Bottom, Left}

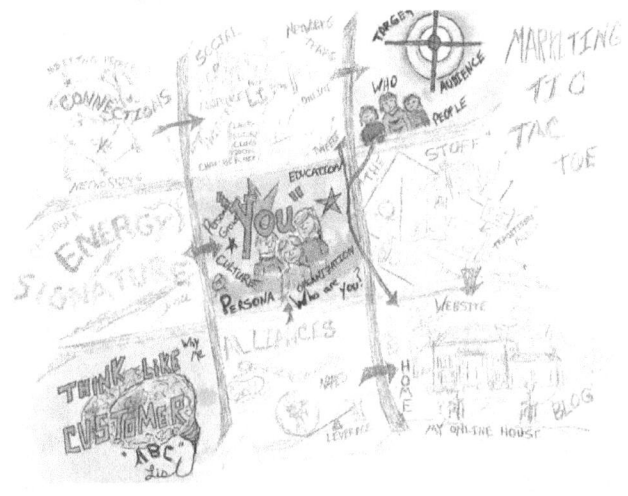

Do you really understand what your customer wants?

Many of us start out in business trying to appeal to the mass market. In our industry that means basic pool designs for basic budgets, nothing really special or unique, but plenty of customers willing to buy what you are building.

If volume is your thing, this business model makes sense.

If you long to provide more creative and custom solutions, you are looking at a smaller, but infinitely more interesting client base. They certainly aren't the typical mass market client with a fixed budget and set expectations as to what "pool" means.

The question becomes: "How can I find a client who is willing to hire me to do this different thing I want to try?"

We believe it's all about telling the right story. What we quickly realized is that our ideal customer is not looking for a pool; rather they are hoping to create a lifestyle experience in their backyard. Once we knew this, we could market to this audience telling stories that could truly resonate. This is where we began to build our voice and our brand story in ways that would appeal to our ideal buyer.

How about you? What does your ideal customer *really* want, and how can you inform your marketing to tell that story? Do they want something nourishing or something scrumptious? Do they want a fast car or transportation from A to B? Do they want to do more or just make it easier/faster?

How much time do you spend thinking like your customer?

The focus of this square is spending some time spotlighting TLC.

In thinking like our customer, we think about specific ways that they would like to be

Organic Marketing ™

communicated with. This reinforces what we just started to discover in our discussion of personalities.

Why is it so important to understand your target personalities? It's critical because all four personalities like to receive information and use social marketing differently.

Most small business websites built today come from the perspective of the website owner or website programmer, not the end user. This is totally backwards and a good web development company should help you avoid this common error. The decision of website design should have nothing to do with the person who owns the website. It should be designed for the end user. When you understand who your client is, you gear everything toward their perspective, and that way, you start thinking like them and putting messages in front of them in the best possible way.

Consider these questions as you begin to think like your customer. Are your customers high-powered business people? If yes, you must think like a Choleric Driver, and make sure the info is presented quickly, easily and concisely.

Do you need to focus more on the Melancholy personality? Then focus on detailed information, white papers, case studies, facts and figures to ease their transition to the buy.

A Sanguine will want the sales process to be engaging, amusing, and fun, so be sure to build your social campaign around this if you target these types. Shiny stuff in this case is great!

For a Phlegmatic, think consistency, and appeal to their pragmatic nature, and realize they are reluctant to take action; focus on the other types and the phlegmatic will eventually engage, maybe.

We also need to understand where each of the different types of personalities will want to spend their time. When you start with your blog as the foundation for your social media strategy, you have the ability to put your blog posts and messages in front of your audience in whichever of the social media sites they prefer. Each of the personality types will have their own favorite. They will use the site that resonates with them the most and where they enjoy spending their time or find value in their time spent.

To begin thinking like your customer, start to speak to your audience. If your messages are well designed for them, they will like and share. If they don't, you have missed your mark. Start asking questions and listening to the answers you receive. Your audience is already telling you everything they need. All you have to do is tune in. Social media is a great place to do this. You can unabashedly eavesdrop on your prospects and see what they are talking about, needing and asking. You can also ask (gasp) your customers what they would like to see.

Revisit the exploration of tuning into your customer often. What are their needs at present, and how are their needs changing? How are your products and services changing to meet your customers evolving needs?

Listen to what they are asking for and fill that specific need with stories relating to the solutions you offer. Remember, to keep in mind when offering your services, your customers they don't want to know how the watch works; they really just want to know the time. It's an old cliché, and applies in the new media more than ever.

Case Study: Furniture Restoration[14]

The middle square of "You," is all about defining yourself. This square is all about defining your target audience and identifying the commonalities and demographic information that will help you in your marketing.

Let's look at this example of a furniture restoration entrepreneur. To begin the process, we looked at the target audience of who would be interested in hiring someone to help them with furniture restoration and antique preservation. The first questions we asked the owner were: Who is his customer? What did his typical client look like?

When considering the target personality, we narrowed his market down to: Women who typically inherit the family furniture and are also

---

[14] Israel Retana was with our InSights Community almost from the beginning and is a great example for this case study.

often concerned with preserving the legacy for future generations.

If this furniture restorer focused on marketing to everyone, including men, women, and children, he would have been wasting much of his efforts. In this case, we began thinking like his customer, and applied the marketing efforts to be focused on women to speak to the legacy and family history they are looking to enjoy and to preserve.

When you are able to apply this thinking, you will be able to narrow down your market to some basic demographics, and then take it a step further into personality types. You can really begin to craft some highly targeted and successful messages. The next step, in our study of the target audience, is to delve into thinking like the customer wanting furniture restoration and factor in their primary personality.

The personality of someone who would be the ideal client for furniture restoration in this case is someone who is sentimental, someone who has a tie to the furniture. They would most likely want to showcase the furniture in their home.

This client would most likely have some discretionary income.

Since furniture restoration is not an impulse purchase it will really be a sentimental purchase. This is going to be a personal decision, where they really feel that doing this will add some value to their life, to their family, to their home, for personal and sentimental reasons.

The antique or inherited heirloom furniture itself has intrinsic value to the client and they are willing to invest in its restoration.

More than likely, the target audience of women would be middle-aged or older. They will reminisce about good times spent at grandmother's house, sitting on that chair, and they may be more sentimental.

Using the personality discovery process, we narrowed our audience from the entire universe to women, to age specific women, to lifestyle specific women. A Choleric personality may want to restore furniture for the individual wow factor. Sanguine personalities will want to for the social value to them, and melancholies will focus on the details and the value of the family history.

Then we honed in on that market and specifically targeted the message to them.

That eliminated a lot of wasted time and energy spent going nowhere and allowed marketing to focus tightly onto a target that would be accepting of the message. It also meant creating messages that they would enjoy seeing, in words they would enjoy to hear. It also meant evaluating which social channels would reach them the best. We will explore more about social channels in future squares.

The Importance of TLC[15]

How often do we, in our over exuberance about our company and service offering, try to share as much information with a prospect as we possibly can?

Do we sometimes share too much? Do we answer the unasked questions and try to justify our position even before we have learned what our customer is looking for?

It is in our nature to share what we know and sometimes in our excitement explain it, sometimes in technical terms, with way too much detail, and raise issues that are important to us[16].

Take the time to listen first and then ask questions of what your audience wants to hear, and then share, share, share.

Remember not to answer the unasked question of your immediate prospect. The ideas and needs of the customer are more important than what we may think they need to know.

---

[15] Thinking Like your Customer

[16]Note that we said things that are important to US, not necessarily important to our customers.

Understanding your Target Audience leads to Niche Marketing

Niche Marketing is when a company or a person understands who they are and what they offer, as a product or service that carefully defines their specialty niche. Successful niche marketing will support that specially chosen niche and will relay that very clearly and concisely to the target audience. This is exactly what our furniture restoration expert was able to do.

Rendall's Tic-Tac-Toe Exploration

Some friends of ours in the business world (and also personally) are the team over at Rendall's Certified Cleaning Company[17], here in Michigan. Rendall's has been an actively marketing company for years, though in the past 12 months they have embraced the Organic Marketing™ Tic-Tac-Toe process in a very noticeable way. They have grown even more attuned to their Certain Way and their ideal client.

Jackie, 3rd generation Rendall's team member shares:

"When asked to TLC, we started with "Kathy." She is a client who we have worked with that seemed to mesh really well with who we are and who we want to work for.

---

[17] www.rendallscleaning.com

We upgraded the name to "Sherry" because of a recent client who has shown us that we can be even more specific about finding our perfect client.

Identifying who they are helps us figure out where they hang out more specifically. Figuring out their passions (there's a trend of our clients who are interested in the same things, i.e. gardening, local food), and the places they shop at (i.e. local family owned stores).

It continues to help us think of being in their shoes and how we can draw these people in specifically with our message, marketing, graphic design, videos, etc."

Scott (2nd generation) adds:

"We are now much more attuned, when we are speaking with new (and existing) clients, to seek whether or not they're a "Sherry" or a "Kathy."

We've done persona marketing for many years, though we lumped them all into a generic category that we called "Sally," who met our age, location, and income bracket—and nothing else.

After doing the tic-tac-toe we discovered that there is much more to our ideal client than just age, location, and income. We know a lot more about her now, the way she thinks and more of what she needs to see in our marketing than we did before, and we discover more things about her as time goes on. While "Sherry" and "Kathy" are also "Sally," they are so much more than Sally.

Defining Your Certain Way

When you have clearly defined your center square of YOU and become clear about your Target Audience, and begin to think like them with a little TLC, you will be able to put messages in front of them that resonate more than they ever have before. This three in a row is a definite win!

Next, we'll move into the Energy Signature that will best represent you and your brand.

Your Energy Signature
{Middle, Left}

Our energy infuses everything we do.

If we aren't happy in our work, how can our customers be?

"Forget about keeping your customers happy. Keep yourself happy in your work and that joy can't help but infuse everything you touch." ~ Al Curtis

I was having a chat with a customer and another contractor on a job site a while ago. The contractor was saying "Oh, for us, it's really important that the customer is always happy."

In front of the customer, I stopped him and said, "I disagree." I explained that I believe if I can find a way to be happy in what I do, then the customer is guaranteed to be happy.

I explained, "If I focus on the customer's happiness and try to do everything according to them, and I am not enjoying the process, and I am not loving the process, then we all miss out because the customer won't be happy either," I continued.

Some customers, to be sure, won't agree to this approach, and we learned the hard way a few years ago that we shouldn't be working for those people. We found saying no is sometimes the most powerful way to find our own happiness and our own joy. For those who get it, these projects are truly a joyful collaboration. The joy transfuses everything we touch, leaving an unforgettable Energy Signature for our brand.

One of our favorite squares in the entire Marketing Tic-Tac-Toe™ process is the Energy Signature. This is such a fun space to develop!

As an example, think of someone who just lights up the room with energy as soon as they enter. Their vibe seems to swirl around them and pick everyone up. This is someone with an exceptional Energy Signature.

Likewise, we all know those people who can bring a room down just by their presence in it. This is their Energy Signature, and one that we may just want to avoid.

We all have an Energy Signature, as do our companies, whether we are conscious of it or not.

The energy that you bring to your work, to your connections and to your social relationships is all a part of your Energy Signature.

When you are not in the room, what are people saying about you, and what are they saying (or feeling) about your company, or the way you do business?

Your Energy Signature is critical in creating a marketing strategy that works. In all of Organic Marketing ™, you want people talking and feeling so especially positively about you they ooze good vibes about you and your company whenever your name comes up.

You will also want to make sure that your Energy Signature is positive, is upbeat, is exciting and is worthwhile to share.

The ideal signature will be when you or your company come up in conversation, or you show up, and the air feels lighter and brighter and excitement happens, that is a great Energy Signature.

The good news is that wherever you find yourself and your Energy Signature right now, you can begin to reshape it for your future, in whichever way you'd like!

In a company or team you can also develop the Energy Signature representative of individuals, and of the entire team. Whether you are in a leadership position or not, people will take their cues from positive and energetic people around them. This is the perfect area to begin to lead by example.

Your positive Energy Signature brings more long-term benefits along with it than anything else you do because it can be present even when you are not.

When you focus on your message, and the Energy Signature that you want to be known for, it can be carried on and shared by others.

Video is an especially great way to share an Energy Signature. When you embrace video creation for yourself and your company, you can share, in your own words, what you do, why you do it, and the viewer can see your energy coming through. The best thing about video is that if the viewer likes what they see, the share buttons on social media make it so simple for them to pass your message along. Then you get the recommendation of a connection, and the new viewer also gets to meet you and experience your energy; all straight from your very own well crafted message!

When we make sure that we craft our message and our Energy Signature so that people want to pass it on, it creates a better potential for us, our company, and our brand.

If we don't do a good job crafting our message, we just add to the confusion and noise that exists in the world where there are so many brands competing for awareness. A solid brand with a clear niche and creative Energy Signature has no competition.

When our message is good, our persona is good, and our Energy Signature is great, we have a winning combination. The person receiving our awesome message can understand it, and in the best case scenario, they will pass it on to their, often like-minded, people as quickly, concisely, and precisely as we did.

A well packaged message with a strong Energy Signature will allow the message to stay uniform and come across strong.

One strategy to consider when developing an Energy Signature is to be just a little bit mysterious. You can share information that will tease people into wanting to know more and create a sense of curiosity.

To do this, and create some mystery and engagement on our Facebook page, we share a little teaser about something we are working on, or announce a surprise coming up soon. You'd be surprised how many people play along, guessing as to what it will be. They also engage others when they share the message to see what ideas their friends may come up with.

Whether you are working on your personal, professional or company Energy Signature, have fun with it and create it with consistency.

Avoid the shotgun approach to social media, where you shoot a little of this and you try a little of that and you do a little bit of something else. You'll get exactly what you put into it. A very haphazard message that is fragmented and confusing. Be consistent, with a strong Energy Signature, and people will be drawn to engage with you.

Making Energy Signature Connections

Making personal connections through marketing is the key to success, especially through the use of photo and video.

When using today's biggest marketing strategies, social media, it is a very good idea to add a photo to your profile. This will help potential customers make better connections to you and your company. When they can see who they are going to be dealing with, it creates a comfortable first meeting because they know who to expect.

Video takes this a step further. Before ever meeting you, a potential customer can get to know you, hear how you sound, find out your approach, and even before the first meeting, evaluate for themselves whether they feel there is a fit.

When we first started sharing our philosophy about photos and video some people embraced it. A few people were skeptical and expressed concern about this type of sharing.

We have found that our customers and business connections love seeing the photos and videos and then see that same person walk into their home. They feel comfortable with us. They feel like they already know us through our photo and video efforts. It is one of the most important things that we have done, and we can't stress that enough, this is a huge piece of a great Energy Signature.

Our visibility in photos and video has not only resulted in our customers finding us but also other industry leaders and even media agents.

At the time of this publishing, our team at *Ask the Pool Guy* has been approached by three separate production companies to get to know us and discuss the possibility of taking our message to a broader audience[18]. One media agent that we spoke with, regarding the possibility of a show, loved the use of photos on our site. He mentioned that of the dozen sites he had recently been on, we were the only one to feature photos of the owner and the team members in such a prominent way and he really appreciated that!

---

[18] Our customers tend to be down to earth and are mostly reluctant to bring that type of attention to their back yards or themselves. We'll see what the future brings, the timing isn't quite right yet. Stay tuned!

If a media company can see this, imagine what your customers see and how they feel about you—the company they can get to know online through your photos and videos.

We can say without hesitation, photos and videos work!

Make some time to reflect on how your Energy Signature comes through your photos and videos.

Think about the impression that you leave with people once they have met you.

How is your Energy Signature working?

When you walk into a room, do you brighten it up or does it become a little dimmer? (If you don't know the answer to this, consider asking a focus group of some of your objective friends and business connections.)

Ask some of your business connections when someone thinks about you, what is the first aspect of your brand that comes to mind?

Try to also find out the answers to these questions:

Do they think about you with positive thoughts? Are you uplifting? Are you a go-to person for support and for your products or services?

Are you a resource within your circle of friends, clients, and contacts?

What are the emotions that your product or service draws out of people?

The answers to these questions should all be considered as parts of your Energy Signature. The great news is that once you recognize the pieces that are at work, you can influence how your Energy Signature comes together and evolves.

Take the time to really get to know your Energy Signature and make every interaction count. Being the most present and authentic version of yourself is the very first step.

Second is telling your story effectively. An effective story will create an emotional response in the reader or listener. People make decisions based on emotion; that is basic human nature. Use this tie in to create the emotional connection with your connections. Your chance of doing business with them, being referred by them, and in general having a great relationship depends on this connection.

Become a motivator within your sphere of influence. The Energy Signature of a motivator is drawing others in, encouraging them, and helping them to get somewhere that they would like to go.

When you leave people in a position that is greater than yourself at the end of your interaction, you have the strongest Energy Signature possible. In Steve Farber's book *Greater Than yourself*[iii], Steve shares just how you can help create long lasting and powerful relationships based on this connection.

Energy Signatures in Action

An Energy Signature creates a baseline interaction for you, even when you are not there.

They let someone know who you are, how you are, and so much more.

A simple example of where your Energy Signature makes a first impression for you is with your outgoing voice mail recording. Is it happy and fun filled, or ordinary and unimpressive? Sandi has often used creative and fun outgoing messages on her voicemail. You wouldn't believe how many people say "wow, that made my day!" before leaving their message.

Were you in a rush when you created it? Do you talk fast, slow, or moderate? How does it make the person on the other end feel when they get it?

All these are questions need to be asked when thinking about your Energy Signature. They all relate to the same thing, priorities. If you are in a rush when you create your voice mail greeting, it gives off the impression that you do not take time and do things thoroughly. If you "phone it in" how creative and energetic are you?

Now imagine you are creating the voice recording for your company, the same way you created your personal voice recording, in a rush and talking very fast. This does not leave your customer excited to talk to you and perhaps they ignore the returning call they get the next day and go find a much happier company, all because of that one voice recording.

The littlest things can impact and give light to the personality and Energy Signature of the entire company.

Energy Signature in Marketing

When you market with your Energy Signature fully engaged, you bring your energy, the energy of your company and your team with you in all of your interactions, whether business, or online in social media.

The next step in developing your Energy Signature will be to make sure you have a face for your business. If you are a solo entrepreneur that includes your smiling face in your marketing efforts. If you have a team, be sure to showcase their photos as well, either individually or in a group photo and video. People do business with people, not a logo.

When you have a face for your company just like Ask the Pool Guy does, your brand becomes so much more recognizable. We have gone as far as having a caricature of Al and Sandi, so we can incorporate those into our marketing mix where most appropriate as well.

We are sure to feature our team members on our website, and in our social media messages and postings so that people can get to know us as people, and not just an anonymous brand that they do business with.

By including our team we become fun and recognizable. There is so much that can be done (with the stuff[19]) when you have fun and engage your company brand identity to enhance an already awesome Energy Signature.

Defining Your Certain Way

When you have clearly defined the center square of YOU, and become clear about your Target Audience, begin to think like them, you will be able to put messages in front of them that make an impact more than they ever have before. Your Energy Signature will reinforce your brand identity and will continue to become an even more important part of everything that you do.

Next, we'll move into how to make and utilize Connections.

---

[19] Upcoming in the Stuff Square, stay tuned!

Connections

{Top, Left}

To build your tribe and gain a following, you have to keep showing up.

> *"In a busy marketplace, not standing out is the same as being invisible."* ~
> *Seth Godin*

Al remembers the moment like it was yesterday.

"I was just leaving Home Depot, with a random sack of fittings for a job, when I spotted a man hanging around my company van. My first thought was "oh great, what is this guy up to?" not sure what he was after, standing next to my well-worn construction van.

As I picked up my pace, puffed out my chest, and donned my best "ready for anything" face, the man saw me coming, broke into a big grin and said "Hey, Pool Guy, I've got a question to ask ya!"

That's when I knew there would be no trouble; I was being sought out for my industry expertise. What a great realization and a fun confirmation that our niche marketing concept was truly working.

As you begin to make connections and build a tribe with your marketing, finding some way to stand out is critical. What can you do/say/be that will make people take notice, remember you, and most importantly, seek you out when they need you?

What makes you more than a face in the crowd?

Connections are a major factor in your Organic Marketing™ Strategy. Your prospects and customers form a tribe in the new marketplace. Seth Godin explains the concept brilliantly in his book, *Tribes*[iv].

Every tribe needs a leader. When you are marketing your business, keep this leadership role in mind. When you truly have a tribe, your followers will be inspired and excited to share your message with others.

When we created the InSights Community, we didn't realize it at the time but, we were forming a new tribe. The members went as far as to call themselves InSights Enthusiasts. They even helped brainstorm the title. The people who believed in our message, who were excited and inspired by what we created, became members of our tribe. To this day, they believe in the organization and in their relationships with each other. Our tribe mates are willing to share our message with others, encouraging others to come see what this positive community is all about. They want to be involved with the community and with individual members.

When we can't be face to face with the members of our tribe in person, we stay engaged with them on Facebook and in our blog. It keeps the relationships growing all the time. This is a part of the continual cultural shift that is happening throughout the world, due in part to social media's ability to connect us in new ways. It is also organic proof of the power of our social graph. Social Media offers a great place to build a tribe, a following of fans and friends, and to share a continual stream of information and engagement and motivation with each other.

Keep in mind that it's not enough to gather followers and friends on Facebook and other social media. To truly make a tribe, you have to give back. There has to be value to your tribe or they will look elsewhere. You can provide this value by giving back, staying connected, "liking" their business pages, commenting on their new threads, and building their network.

Offer resources and share, covering WIIFM (What's in it for me?) this can be as simple as the good feelings generated by paying it forward to support and recognition for their efforts.

Whenever appropriate, make online introductions between members of your tribe. Personal and business introductions are a fantastic way to do this, and to give back to the people who support you.

During this part of the discussion, we are asked to distinguish between a tribe and a crowd. Let us explain the distinction with of a circus and a concert experience.

At a circus, you find a group of people who are going to have fun and be entertained. That is a crowd. On the other hand, if a specific event is targeted to a group of "fans" like a musical concert, the people attending will be excited about that particular musician. This is where you might find yourself in the middle of a tribe. They are there for the common experience. They are more invested in and excited about the event. They "believe" in it. This was apparent as Al and his lifelong friend Moe attended a recent Eagles Concert. The concert goers were an enthusiastic tribe, and the band rewarded the tribe by giving their all during the performance, just as they have for all these years. As Al shares, it was truly a magical experience.

A tribe is a group of people who are willing to be a part and support a movement based on the leadership of that tribe.

Your tribe is where you will find much of your business support. It is important to constantly nurture and build your tribe, some may become customers, and even more importantly they will share you with others. Create enjoyment and encourage the sharing of your messages with their connections. The result is that your business will grow.

Creating your ABC list (for entrepreneurs)

How do we identify and create this tribe that will help support our business efforts? The number one thing that we all need to do is identify your ABC list.

To gain an understanding of you're A-B-C Sphere, sit down, by yourself or with your team, and write down every person's name that you know, whether they are close (true friends and family), distant (you happen to meet them at a networking event and got one of their cards), or somewhere in between (neighbors, classmates, the mom in your PTO group, etc). Facebook, as it happens, does this beautifully, as do Linked-In and Twitter. The old fashioned Rolodex or address book do this as well.

Next, break it down. Assign every name an "A" "B" or "C" value. Your A List contains the people who if you called would drop what they are doing to come to your aid. They are going to listen or to help you. They already believe in you and what you stand for. For your business associates on your A List, you would be comfortable referring one of your clients to them or they would be comfortable referring someone to you, and you each know that the client would be taken care of.

Your B List includes the people who know what you do. They may know a lot or a little about you. They would speak to you on the street, and would maybe know your name or a little bit about your family or business. You don't quite have the relationship with them as you do your A-Lister's. You are comfortable dealing with them and engaging them.

Your C List will be the rest of those people on the list who know you by name, even if only distantly. Maybe they only recognize you if you are wearing a name tag. They may not even remember what you do for work. If you bumped into them, there would be some connection.

A large company or small business can identify the ABC lists through considering various spheres of influence, including client lists, email lists, and general inquiry lists. Many CRM[20] (Customer Relationship Management) programs will allow you to track data and glean

---

[20] Try Quickbooks Data Reports as well as HighRiseHQ.com

from reports who the strong members of your tribe are from your customer database. This data is *gold.*

Creating your ABC List will take a little time to create and decipher; put effort into it and really think this through. Don't overlook your alumni connections, your old neighborhoods, home town, past employers – all of these can be gold mines of people who know, like, and trust you.

With your ABC List complete, it's time to start marketing via storytelling. Begin with your A List. It will be the easiest to reach this audience. They will love anything you put out. The members of this list have the strongest connection to you.

Next, begin to connect with your B list with the intention of getting to know them better. Create video messages geared at letting them get to know you better and encourage their curiosity to discover more about you with the intent of moving them from the B list to the A list. Connect more closely with them, earn their trust, and learn more about them. Social media is a great tool in making these connections closer and stronger. Remember, you are building your relationships, not selling directly.

Finally, you'll move on to address through video, blog posts and social shares, your C List and begin to work them onto your B list. In this way, your list is always evolving, becoming more viable and more effective.

Other methods of ABC movement can happen through several different media—the Internet, phone calls, and one-on-one meetings. The bigger the A-List is, the stronger your business. It really is that simple...

Making Connections via Social Networks

The importance of video is moving people along your ABC list. That is exactly the course people take with us at *Legendary Escapes*. By the time they meet us, they have already moved from C's to B's and are getting to know us. Often we find out they came across our website or one of our videos and began to watch our playlists. One family even spent Saturday mornings watching The Pool Guy as a family, even before they chose to work with us. To say that sale was simple is an understatement. They chose Al and our team before he even walked through the door. That is the magic of the ABC process in action.

By the time we meet them they have become our people simply by watching our stuff.

This Square is all about connections and social media is the perfect avenue to enhance these relationships via connections. We consider social media to be all online communication via social sharing and video sharing sites.

You want to meet and connect via social networks where you can identify your friends, and friends of friends; this will allow you to seek out and communicate with new people who do not know you yet. In this square, it is also critical to think about reconnecting with the people who you already know, and may have fallen out of touch.

To the people who say that, "I don't have any time for social media," consider this: You have been using traditional methods of contact to reach out to your existing client base, whether via snail mail, phone calls, radio, or TV. You spend a lot of time, effort, energy, and money to connect with the people on your list.

With social media, when you have grown your sites appropriately, with the push of one button you can interact with those people instantly, when it may have taken hours of phone calls or thousands of dollars before.

Which site deserves your time? What Social Media Tool do you choose? It depends on who you decide to focus on in your target audience square that will help you determine where your customers are. Each social media platform has its particular strengths and that attracts people who enjoy the interface. If you are dealing with B2B (Business to Business) contacts, LinkedIn, Twitter, and Facebook are great in that order. For B2C (Business to Consumer) engagement it is best to start with YouTube, Facebook, possibly Houzz, Pinterest and other specialty sites. You can always use your specialty sites to share to Facebook as well, repurpose and cross promote your content.

We took a quick survey in a recent mastermind meeting and here are the favorites we have in the group:

Sandi's favorite social media site is Facebook. For her it blends fun and personal posting with interesting things to learn and see around the world. For our pool company, we can share photos each day from the job, galleries of projects, and videos. Using Periscope and YouTube we give tours of what we are working on. Facebook is a great place to share our pool company content.

Al also enjoys Facebook because it an easy way to connect for someone who may have limited time throughout the day. It's always with him on his phone and interaction with a like, a comment or a share, is only a click away.

Our friend, Ask the Garden Gal[21], Jodi likes Instagram[22] (she is very sanguine) and loves the quick and simple photo sharing with or without the filters that make things look so cool.

Our friend and Realtor Dave likes Facebook because the business page helps him get things out to people. He also likes Pinterest (also

---

[21] Facebook.com/AsktheGardenGal

[22] *Instagram* is a free and simple way to share your life and keep up with other people. Take a picture or video, then share!

sanguine!) because of the neat things and views of things shared on there.

Stephan[23] loves Pinterest (he is a maker) because of the wealth of ideas shared there. He will take a box of random parts and recycle these pieces of treasure into Steampunk art! Pinterest is the best site for gaining and sharing visual ideas.

If you need to start your social media strategy, now is the time. We recommend your first step is to launch on a blog platform, we recommend WordPress[24]. From your blog you can easily publish and automate your posts and stories to all of your social media sites. This way you can spend some time interacting on the sites you like and still have your message in front of the people who frequent other sites.

When determining where to focus your time it may be helpful to consider some information about the demographics of each of the sites. What is the age of the average user? Using the Facebook ads system you can find how many men vs. women are within a radius of a zip code and craft messages specifically to those users. It

---

[23] ArtSmithCraftWorks.com, he is a maker of Steampunk Air Ships and other amazing art!

[24] Any web host should support self hosted Wordpress, we like Bluehost.com. They don't pay us to say that, we have just used their terrific service for years.

would make sense to create a strategy, considering who your target customer is, and who the bridges to those customers will be. This can help you determine how to allocate your time and resources across the social sites.

Start with your target audience of your favorite (current or potential customers). Ask them what their favorite social site is, and what type of posts they enjoy the most.

Social sharing allows you to share your content that will remain where your audience can find it. Your connections may not always see your message the first time around; nor will they see every note that you post. If you are consistently present on the sites you use, they will have a higher likelihood of seeing your messages. Keep the info fresh and varied and you will very soon have their attention.

A common misstep people make, when thinking about this square in the social media philosophy, is that social media is all about new connections. It's not. It is just as important in re-establishing contact with the relationships that you already have.

As Sandi explains, I can show up to a networking event or group that I have not been to before and I will likely already know three, four, or ten people in the room. Many times, I have only been introduced to them via social media, but it feels like we already know each other. Sometimes if they have watched our videos they will feel like they know me even more, so be prepared with a smile to become fast friends with new connections.

In the social media world, we are able to share enough information with each other, including our photos for facial recognition (back to physiognomy) and bits of our personal stories. This helps them get to know our persona brand.

Once we meet face-to-face, the feeling is like reconnecting with an old friend we haven't seen in a while, rather than meeting someone brand new. This is powerful business networking and relationship building.

When you are making connections in the social media world, be on the look-out for new strategic connections. When you create a significant sphere of influence, people listen to what you have to say because they come to know that you are relevant, entertaining, and informative. You have credibility, and you have influence.

To create even more impact in finding others with similar influence to yours in both your industry and others, begin talking about each other, and suddenly you have the ability to create a new sphere of people who will learn about both of you. Surround yourself with strong influencers, and share your influence with them. That is leveraging your social sphere.

Those individual spheres of influence are the critical elements in leveraging the messaging power of a large organization. A CEO of a company has his/her own sphere of influence. When he or she sends a message out, via their connections in their sphere, a certain amount of people will hear that message and find out about it. That message can then be packaged and travel via all of their team members' social media sites. Individual spheres of influence are now exponentially more powerful and can reach infinitely more people. This type of messaging is something every organization with a team of people needs to deploy.

Our Gary Vaynerchuk Story as told by Sandi

I received an email one day from my friend Colin[25] who sent me a link to a keynote presentation by Gary Vaynerchuk of Wine Library TV. He sent this link because he thought I'd be interested in a comment from the audience at the end. Gary was giving a keynote speech in Las Vegas about monetizing some aspects of online businesses.

In the audience that day, there was a woman, Gail[26], who was launching a free hugs campaign. She was raising money for charity to travel around the world and deliver hugs to different countries. While they were stopping and delivering hugs, they were going to donate to various charities along the way.

---

[25] Colin Thomas, Brighton, MI An internet savvy friend...

[26] Gail Lynne Goodwin, inspiremetoday.com

After the keynote presentation, Gail stood up to ask a question. She asked Gary what was one of the ways that she could use social media to promote her free hugs campaign. That answer is why my friend Colin thought of sending this link to me.

I have my own story about Free Hugs[27] here at the InSights Community. Colin recognized a story I would enjoy, so he shared it with me. I went to the website of the woman who spoke on the video about her Free Hugs campaign. As it turns out, I was already connected to her on Twitter. I was able to visit her website, leave a comment on one of her posts, and offer some support for her Free Hugs campaign.

About a week later, I was reading the book *Tribes* by Seth Godin. In the book, Seth Godin profiles none other than Gary Vaynerchuk from Wine Library TV. Coincidence, it was the second time in a week that Gary Vaynerchuk came up in front of me. Since I was blogging about social success at the time, I began a new blog post telling the story of the sequence of events leading me to notice the second connection to Gary.

Within about six hours of publishing that blog post, Gail, the woman who had been in the audience at the presentation, left a comment about her campaign and thanked us for linking to

---

[27] See the story in the appendix.

it and showing some support. I now had a connection with a woman who is bringing a Free Hugs campaign around the world. If I decided that I wanted to meet up with them in Istanbul, I would have a connection; we have already broken the ice. I know who she is and she knows who I am. We have a connection that we would not have without social media.

The rest of this story gets even better. Planning a trip to New York to see Seth Godin, we decided to send Gary an e-mail to say that we'd be in town and to find out if he'd have some time for us. He said yes and we spent an afternoon touring Wine Library and talking with Gary about his perspectives. It was a great time and we wouldn't have made that connection if not for Social Media.

We connected with Gary Vaynerchuk, who we have followed since his Wine Library TV days, while on a trip to New York City to visit Seth Godin and the launch of his book Linchpin.

Social Media and your Career

We have lived through a cultural shift in the way marketing is done, and the way people are communicating. We have also witnessed instances where social media has become one of the leading criteria in the hiring process.

Employers are increasingly interested in how you are represented in the social media. They are looking at the amount of influence you have in your industry, your region, and your larger community. They also look at how team members are representing themselves online.

Whether you are an entrepreneur or a future college grad, developing your sphere of influence is an essential part of today's world and it is all about making connections.

Consider this: children from circa 2008 and on (the social media era), are growing up with their own Facebook accounts. Until this recent generation, most people would go through their lives—schools, cities, careers—without a method of remaining in contact with most of those that they met. It took great effort to stay in touch with people once you left school, a job or moved to a new state.

The ability to remain connected has radically changed the way we relate to people throughout our lives. Through their social spheres, now, the next generations start building their sphere of influence at an early age. They will take that sphere of influence with them throughout life. Imagine if you were still in touch, in some way, with just about everyone you ever met. This generation will be. The power that this has in our future business and personal endeavors is incredible.

The time is now to begin building your sphere, wherever and whenever you can. You don't have to start from the beginning and try to have everything in place all at once. We are proponents of leaning into the process. Wherever you find yourself today with social media is the right place for you to start.

If you have people around you who are not yet using social media, this is the perfect time for you to help educate them as to why it is so important and you can help them discover the importance of working on their own social graph.

While you embrace social media, follow a clear social media strategy, especially if you'd like to be effective in business. Here's a suggestion of *what not to* do from Sandi:

"We've all seen the requests: change your profile picture to a favorite cartoon, flower, animal, or even logo. Sometimes these requests come wrapped in a "cause," other times it's just for fun.

I am all for supporting worthy causes. What I am not so interested in is seeing the peer pressure generated by social networking sites that encourage a random action. If you want to really support a cause, share a link to that cause via your social media sites, where someone can click a button and DO something—donate money; sign up to volunteer, sign a petition. Really, anything other than just changing a profile picture or doing a silly stunt would be of benefit.

I will not change my profile picture this week to my favorite canine friend, in the guise of helping animals. I do support a lot of causes and, when appropriate, share them via my social media sites. Think twice about following your peers. Be sure, that if you choose to follow along, it fits your Energy Signature and your overall strategy.

Defining Your Certain Way

When you have clearly defined the center square of YOU, and become clear about your Target Audience, begin to think like them, you will be able to put messages in front of them that are effective. Your Energy Signature will become an even more important part of everything that you do, you will be able to make and utilize connections.

Next, we'll move into Social Networks and Relationships and begin to use online media.

Your Social Networks & Relationships

{Top, Middle}

When you find the right niche, and share your clients thoughts via video, new clients select themselves to work with you.

Referrals are the Holy Grail in any kind of service industry. Getting a personal recommendation from someone you've worked with is magic in terms of easing the sales process

109

toward "yes" the next time around. In our case we capture our favorite and most enthusiastic homeowners on video so in their own words they can explain us and working with us to new prospects.

Our adventure into hybrid pools began years ago when a customer wanted a traditional vinyl liner pool, and also wanted to put deck chairs in the shallow end and have a swim-up bar with stools that would sit in the water—possibly tearing the liner and causing expensive repairs.

Al suggested a combination of two traditional pool building techniques; the body of the pool would be done with a traditional vinyl liner, and the sun shelf plus swim-up bar and table area would be crafted in gunite. The clients absolutely loved the idea and our career in hybrid pools was launched.

Because of our commitment to thinking creatively and offering true solutions, and sharing it all via video, new inquiries for what we do seem to take care of themselves. We have been able to take our pick of exciting and challenging projects. As more homeowners see these awesome hybrid pools online, the general feeling seems to be "It's gorgeous! I want one!"

That is the best kind of lead in you can ask for. When you end a project with happy customers and amazing work, what do you do to build on that momentum?

Are you using those relationships to build your business in a tangible way?

This square is all about sharing your message with your social networks. Your social networks include your online and offline networks. These can include sports clubs, social clubs, political organizations, and many more. We will spend quite a bit of time discussing the trends of developing online social media networks, but don't short change your in-person networks as well.

Your brand and persona shared via social channels will include your face, name, and title or tag line (your catchy marketing phrase).

It is not so much a personal brand as it is a *persona brand*.

Persona Branding and your Social Relationships

With the addition of our social relationships, this square begins to combine elements of our center square of you, your Energy Signature, and persona brand.

If you are a solo entrepreneur or small business owner, the center square started with is YOU, personally, and you need to embrace your persona in your social sharing and storytelling.

If you are a large corporation or part of a larger company, that center square starts with the culture of your company, the personas of the brand and your people, your mission, your vision, and your message. Your social sharing will need to contain all of that plus your team members for the most personable interactions.

The difference between personal and persona is that your persona brand is how you represent yourself to the outside world. It takes on characteristics that you decide deliberately to share, versus everything that is you on a personal level.

When we balance personal with persona in business, we are able to share the best, most effective parts of ourselves and our message with our business connections and keep our personal details off the radar.

How do I use social media for business the best way, do it effectively, and not over share? These are the biggest questions that come up, and often hinder the social media campaigns of individuals and businesses. To help you frame your persona brand which will be crafted especially for social sharing, start by giving some thought to these questions:

What is your "Why"? What is your intention? What is the reason that you are doing what you do? What is the intent that you have for people who will ultimately work with you?

Taking this further, is your purpose on purpose? Is everything that you are doing in the day-to-day marketing and operations of your business on track with your Why?

What is the culture of your business? When people think of doing business with you, do you have a strong culture, and business essence? Is your culture fun and exciting or is it melancholy and boring? Are people drawn toward you? Obviously if you are not quite as fun and exciting as you'd like to be, you have some room for growth and creative thinking.

We have had some interesting case studies. Believe us, if we can make dentistry, carpet cleaning and trench digging exciting, there is room for whatever you do.

What elements of your personality, both individually and as part of the team, must be a part of your persona brand? If you or your company has some signature traits, you can bet that those are part of your persona. Allow those to be represented and encouraged when it comes to the promotion of your business culture and identity in your Organic Marketing™ process. As consumers, people want to know what is specific and special about you and your business. This is your greatest asset (and your secret sauce!)

Strive for your social messages to be a mix of business and more personable stories.

Most importantly when it comes to motivation for sharing anything that you or your company is doing it is to ask yourself the question, "Are you chasing your bliss?" You know the answer is yes when no matter what you are doing, time seems to stand still and it's almost effortless to be doing what you are doing. Strive to create and experience more of these moments, and even capture some to share. This positive energy will translate into business success. During our busy days, we don't always take the time to appreciate the moments. We need to remember on a daily basis to do or think about what makes us blissful and what makes us the happiest, and share those moments!

These questions may be easy to answer and define if you are an entrepreneur or solo-preneur. If you have a team of people working together, the company persona will be influenced collectively by the personas of each person within the organization. This is a great time to check on your team to make sure you have the right people in the right seats developing your messages. Define your culture and make sure everyone in the organization fits within that culture.

Let's take the next step in our persona brand development and relate it to social media. To build the social media foundation of your brand, look at your Why and how you will incorporate these into your social media presence.

As a member of a company or organization, you may need to hold some Organic Marketing™ strategy and focus meetings on how you craft a persona for the company, so that everyone is working from the same message. As you utilize the strengths within your team to help support your social media strategy, make sure that every individual understands the focus of the company. Be sure you all understand:

Why is this organization participating in social media?

What are the types of conversations we are going to have on behalf of the company? What is our Energy Signature?

What are the types of conversations that we will be taking on ourselves when personally interacting with people?

We can't stress enough how getting the center square (YOU) right is critically important to influence how this message and strategy begins to come together.

If you understand who you really are and what your message is, it is so much easier to share your story.

A solid center square starts with understanding the company's *Why*, the mission and vision, and why it is important to each member of the team.

Effective social media engagement requires transparency and complete authenticity coming from every voice speaking on your behalf. You need a clear, uniform message going out into the world, based on your culture and persona brand.

When the culture of your company and brand is shared effectively in your social media, it will leave a lasting impression of who you are. If your culture is fun, exciting, different, bold, new, fresh ... that will stick in people's minds. Sharing your culture means everything. Make sure that your energy translates into your memorable Energy Signature. It all works together. Having a great culture leads to a great Energy Signature which leave a lasting impression. Empowering the personas within your people creates a great organization.

The Power of Social Relationships

Social relationships can take on any number of forms. While perhaps the most common way we relate is via our Facebook "Friends," we have to expand the definition of "socializing" to fully integrate the concept into an Organic Marketing™ strategy.

The profiles you create on social media sites are a significant piece of this social relationship. If your profile depicts you as a person with strong interests and a solid, consistent persona, it gives you credibility. If you think, "I am just going to throw a profile up on all of these sites because it is something that I have been told to do," your results will be less than stellar.

Al has a nephew who said, "You know, I don't really want to do that social media thing ... I don't want people to know anything about me." He is now a recent college grad, looking for a job, and is probably wondering, "Hmm ... I wonder why it is a little more difficult to get in the door?" The answer lies in his connections, or in this case, obvious lack of them. We can all write a resume and give our credentials to try to get into the door the old-school way. But understand that the easiest and more effective way to be introduced to a company or an organization in this new economy is through your sphere of influence. Beyond that, an employer today is also going to look up a persons' social media profile to get a real-time understanding of their character and how they interact in the world.

116

Jobs are being found (and opportunities are being lost) every day based on this.

Those who get involved now, create authentic profiles, and build large spheres of influence will have a much easier time in the future because they already have a base to operate from. If someone tries to get a start later on, they will be that much further behind than if they start right now. Be a timely adapter, create those relationships and begin to leverage them in everything you do from here forward.

There are many, many sites where you can become involved with social media. You do not have to have a profile on every single one and you do not have to spend time on every single one. Once you become more comfortable with social media, you can add sites as you go, and automate and streamline the experience. For now, we recommend you start with YouTube, and these three: Facebook, LinkedIn and Twitter. You can also add, Instagram, Houzz, Pinterest and others as they come out and you start to discover more of where your audience is spending their time.

Think about this: If you start today, to build a larger sphere of influence in the social media world, what will you have in five years? If you do a little bit today and a little bit tomorrow and you connect with people from your past and you connect with all the people you are associated with in "real life," where do you see yourself in five years? How much social clout could you command? How could you influence opinions, be a leader, or act as a change agent?

Let's say it is five years from now and you are looking for a new job. The hiring manager says "tell me about your social media network." If you have been building your sphere for the past five years, you could easily say "Well, I have 100,000 connections on Twitter, 3,000 connections on Facebook, and I am connected in LinkedIn with 1,500 people in my industry." your potential employer knows that you have spent your time building a sphere of influence, which creates tremendous potential for them. Not only that, if that employer senses that you will be a great team player and social sharer for the brand, and are willing to leverage your social media presence on behalf of the company, you've got a winning combination.

Let's explore leveraging a social network. A company takes on social media and commits to creating social media presence. What happens when you reward people for building a social media sphere of influence? Klout[28] has come on the scene to measure exactly that. We can certainly see a future in which raises will be based on this sphere of influence that you create and your willingness to share your brand with your networks. Conversely, we can see your

---

[28] Klout.com, measures your online impact on a scale of 1-100

employer making strategic team decisions and deciding they may not need you anymore if your social sphere remains small and doesn't help spread the company's message. In some cases your social media is a sad case of poor judgment. Avoid that at all costs.

Start today to create your sphere. If you take some time every day to build your connections and social relationships, you will create conversation today and opportunities tomorrow. Let's say three years from now you decide to try something new and open a new business venture. You now have a ready-made sphere of influence you can leverage in the future. They already know, love, and trust you, and they will be willing to listen to what you have to say. When you decide to bring out a new product, share a new service, or promote your brand expansion, you have a built-in audience.

The companies that create a great strategy, and that can subtly grow their social media to the point where it is influential, will softly create a market through the process of leveraging their social graph without having to scream out to the world, "Hey, buy from me." If you start to pay attention to the psychology of how it is used, any corporation, whether small or large, can tap into this amazing potential[29].

---

[29] Refer to Our Certain Way (2015) for examples of this from our brand story!

Social Media Campaign

Once you have created your profiles (starting with FB, LI and TW), you can begin to implement a strong social media campaign based on a strategy for interaction.

First, you have to start with a good grasp of what you want to accomplish on social media. Are you looking to build your ABC List? Do you want more fans? Are you hoping to spread your content? Are you looking for new ways to talk to your customers? Knowing why you want to engage on social media is the first step.

The most important thing to remember is social media is not about your company; social media is about you. Refer back to the center square and what we referred to as persona branding. Good social branding begins with building the brand of you, including your name, your face, who you are, and what you do. Your "Why" of what you do should be the foundation. Once you put this together, it comes across as a complete package. Rather than leading with your company name, lead with your face and your name. That is what people will recognize and remember.

Social Media is like a Party

To help people understand how to begin to interact effectively via social media, Al relates how social media is like a party.

Imagine it is a Friday night and you have been invited to a social event. Maybe you know people there; maybe you don't. You show up. Are you showing up to sell yourself to people? Are you hoping they will buy something from you tonight? Or are you showing up there socially, to meet new people, have some fun, to interact, and build stronger relationships? Most people going to social events are there to do exactly that—socialize, just get together and talk and have fun and meet new people. Social media is the same way, except this is an online party, with millions of guests.

Once the party is over and you decide that you met someone who you think is interesting or cool, the question becomes how to get to know them better. What should you do? What's the logical next step? It would be to invite them to the party at your house next.

In getting to know them, you extend an invitation to your party, which in the social world is your online house. This can be your website, your blog, your Facebook profile or page; any place they can visit to learn more about you. Your new friend can then decide, "Am I interested in this person and what they are doing? Are they an interesting person sharing interesting things?"

Let's look at the psychology of this for a moment. If we take this time to help people learn about us, and not sell them anything, you may be asking, how does this help our business? The goal with social media and Organic Marketing™

is that we want people to talk about who and what we are, so when the right person needs our product or service we are the first person or company that comes to mind.

Your social presence needs to be engaging. Online, you have very few moments to capture someone's attention. We live in a busy world, and this online space moves like a rocket. This is why your online house needs to get people engaged in your website, quickly and repeatedly.

A good social media plan is to communicate "out loud." Share your conversations that can contribute to your online persona brand out loud. If you belong to a group, and you plan to meet someone there, mention it beforehand via a post on their wall or a status update. Mention the events that you have been going to and who you met there.

Talk to your friends about the type of business that they are in, the type of clients that they service. You can ask some of those leading questions that will encourage people to talk about themselves. Instead of putting out the reasons why people should do business with you, wait until you are asked and hold those conversations with other people.

When someone asks, "So what is it that you do?" you now have permission to put that information out on your wall. If you just start putting your information out and pushing sales content, it is a turn off. If you do too much promotion, chances are that people will tune you out, or possibly un-friend you. Be aware of protocol and expected behaviors on each site so you can maximize your impact and minimize what may not be popular behavior.

Social Relationships on Facebook

Facebook is like a 24-hour news channel and *People Magazine* all rolled into one, and it's all about the people we know. When we create our online sphere of influence through our various accounts, we open a portal into people's lives. This can be personal or professional and it often bridges both. It can cover business or recreation, and often many aspects in between.

As the largest and most popular social media site today, Facebook blends people's personal and professional interests in a new and intriguing way. Through our connections, we get a glimpse of the personal side of people with whom we do business. At the same time, we learn more about the careers of our friends and family members. Our profiles incorporate both the brick and mortar aspects of our business lives, and the more warm and fuzzy elements of our personality.

There are several elements you want to keep in mind if you are using Facebook for business promotion. First and foremost is your profile picture. Make sure it's a good one. Post a clear head shot that features your smile, your face, so that people can quickly and easily see who the profile is about. We call it "leading with your face" and it's an important aspect of good persona branding. Post the family dog photos and the vacation pix in your albums; keep that profile picture just about you.

Why is a headshot so important? It comes down to a scientific understanding of how our brains function[30]. In general, when we look at text, our brain processes the words as information. When we see pictures, we add more bridges between the information and the relationship. To prove this, just look at a class photo from your elementary school years. Chances are you'll remember who in that group you counted as your friends, even if you can't remember their names. Allow people to create a relationship with you, whether you are there in person or not. Your picture will help to make you real. It will make you more engaging, and by nature, someone will want to find out more about you. Chances are that they'll remember more as well.

Facebook Profile or Facebook Page?

Your Facebook profile is your personal space. The information that you share in your profile should be done so it helps people find out about you. You don't want it to read like a business brochure. On your Facebook profile, an under-utilized area for business professionals is the

---

[30] Back to Physiognomy!

"information section." Use the space. Instead of talking about "enjoying walks on the beach and sunny days," put something interesting or catchy in there about your business. When someone runs across your status update or a comment on another post, what you've said there may grab their interest. They'll go to your profile to learn more about you. So this is a great space to utilize to help build your business identity.

Another important section is in your information tab. Fill it out as completely as possible. Add your phone number, email address and a live link to your website or blog. We are always surprised how often we meet someone via social media and try to find their contact information, only to realize it's nowhere to be found. Don't be that person.

Facebook: Pages

While your Facebook profile is your personal space, your Facebook Page is for your business. Pages are a great place for you to create that landing page within the Facebook site that serves as a home page for your business. You can post pictures from recent events, display your logo (or ideally, your plogo), and share information on what types of projects you are doing and with whom.

A huge benefit of social media and blog post automation via an RSS feed is that you can link your blog to your Facebook pages and to your Facebook profile. As you publish a post, it publishes onto Facebook seamlessly this way. This creates a continued avenue for you to gain top-of-mind awareness. Strive to create a balance of business posts and personal conversation starters. Develop a ratio that works for your readers.

If you have a Facebook page or profile, be present every day. Once a week just is not enough time to be present and truly build relationships in your social sphere. Even a couple times a day might be warranted, depending on your audience. If needed, write it on your schedule. If you take the time to plan a strategy, you can put the elements together so they work for you 24/7.

BufferApp[31] is a great way to automate content from your blog and around the web to your sites. You can set and monitor your outgoing posts. Keep an eye out for responses and questions, don't just set it and forget it. You also need to remember to monitor! Be timely with answers and follow up information.

Facebook: Events

The Events feature within Facebook can be a great tool for business promotion. If you are a speaker and you have a seminar coming up, it is

---

[31] BufferApp.com, making social updates simpler to manage.

a great place for you to invite people. What about if you are not a speaker? What if you are not someone who would typically be holding an event? There are some very creative ways to utilize the events feature. Let's look at an example if you are a homebuilder. Create an open house event for a home you are working on. Tell people (via event invitation and social media) that you are going to be at the house at 123 Main Street, and the date and time. (Arrange this with the homeowners first!) Let people know they can stop in on Monday from 2-4 p.m. Invite all to come and ask questions, learn something new about home building, maybe pick up a hammer. It doesn't matter if anybody shows up to that event or not. Chances are you will get a couple people, but more importantly, your friends on Facebook will see that you are active. Take photos and videos of you at the house and of course anyone that stops in to visit you. Get creative and use the opportunity to take video of features, and how you feel about the project. Get observations from people who stop by, and interview your homeowners! Now you have an event, photos, and video for follow up and future social storytelling!

Sharing via social media is all about storytelling. It is sharing what you are doing, where you are, and where people can find you. It is also capturing all of that even when no one is around so they can get to know you and learn more about you. You need to understand the tools so you can use the tools. Events are a great way for you to do some of that type of promotion.

The Art of the Facebook Re-Share

Another way to leverage Facebook is to find information that you can share with your contacts. This doesn't have to be information you originate, it can be sharing messages that are created by other people, brands and organizations. Share, re-share and re-post the messages that other people are posting that you find interesting. If you are hosting an event, send out a note to your friends, "Please share this ... please visit the events tab and post this to your profile." Many people use Facebook as their new source today. The speed and variety of information delivery on Facebook is growing every day. We are learning incredible new things daily, based on interesting things that other people come across and that they share with us: new trends in social media, new websites that are starting up, new products that are on the market, new videos that inspire us to be greater. Be on the forefront of where people are sharing and engaging this information.

Here's one of the most important things to remember about social media, especially on Facebook. If you do too much promotion, people will shut you down. It is regulated by the people using it and the dreaded "unfriend this person" is just a click away. Engage, share, inform, communicate ... and do not sell. If someone asks, you can answer, but do not use Facebook, or any social media site, as a place to pitch.

5 Facebook Reminders

Rule 1: Know the difference between Profiles and Pages

Set up a Facebook Page for your business, and use your Profile for personal connections. This is one of the most important things for you to do. Don't create a personal profile and then forget to be personal. You especially don't want to name it ABC Company and try to use it that way. For starters, it's against Facebook policy; not only that, but people won't pay any attention to you if you try to handle it that way. If you do have a Page for business, you still want to allow as many people as you can to feel like they know you by having the opportunity to be your 'friend.' They'll feel more connected to you here than if they just 'like' your page. So let them. It's good for business.

Also, make sure you add your website to your business page and your personal profile. When people are clicking around to get to know you, make sure they can follow the trail to what you do for business. It's also going to be good for Google and the search engines to recognize this link.

Rule 2: Pay attention to your connections, make small talk

Whether they are your personal profile friends or your connections that like you on your business page make sure you take the time to make conversation.

Think of your online presence like a party, and people keep coming and going. Stop by each group and engage for a moment or two. Ask a question, pop in with a short story, share a photo. The more you are chatty, the more they will be too. That's great for relationship building, top of mind awareness, and it's a lot of fun too!

Pages typically take some getting used to. It's easy to head over to your profile page, visit the feed and see what your friends are up to. It takes initiative on your part to also visit your business page and take the time to make a comment. By nature on Facebook, users want to interact with people, not just a logo, so know that it will take more work to replicate the personal feel on your Facebook page. Be deliberate about the things that you post, and try to make it feel like you are there – in both your profile and on your page. If you have a team that is generating content for your page, feature them in the photos you share, and especially in the photo of the page. It will help – trust me!

Rule 3: Be a Timely Poster

Your connections will each have their own online preference. Watch for trends. When are most of your friends available to chat? Do you see more going on during the day, at night, or on weekends? If you schedule posts automatically from your blog, consider having it post at peak hours for your audience, when it will have more chances of being seen. If you have a schedule to adhere to yourself, consider spending your time on Facebook in the evening – you're likely to bump into more of your friends that way.

Your business page will probably see more daytime traffic than evening or weekend. Plan some well-placed updates to share and keep them early to mid-day. Most people will pay more attention to business matters earlier in the day when they see them.

Rule 4: Mix it up!

If you only share text posts, and say the same thing day after day, your friends will notice – or worse yet, stop noticing! Keep it fresh. Vary your content by using videos, text and photos. There are plenty of status update ideas out there. You can share content from your blog, other blogs, YouTube, a host of other video sources, fun facts, figures and pictures. If variety is the spice of life, think of your status update section as a rotating spice rack. Mix in the variety!

Pay attention! Some of your content will get better engagement (more likes and comments) than others. Watch for trends and share more of what is popular. You should also realize that some people are lurkers. They will watch and read everything you post but may never comment. That's okay. Just realize they are thinking of you when they read your updates, so think of them when you post!

Rule 5: Be Smart about how you Promote

You are probably still reading this book because you understand that you can create amazing new relationships on Facebook and it can be especially good for business. The open forum is a great place to engage with one person, sharing stories, or results of the day, only to be overheard by another person who could really use your services.

What not to say: "Come buy my stuff" or any variation of that theme.

What to say and do:

- ✓ "Helped another awesome client today"
- ✓ "Loved networking to meet new business professionals in my community"
- ✓ "Had a great day playing in the mud[32]!"

---

[32] Okay, that might be pool company specific...you know what we mean!

✓ Thank a colleague for help you got on a project
✓ Give a shout out (thanks) to your graphic designer for help on the new marketing piece you have
✓ Share your excitement for what you are working on
✓ Post a photograph you like that is relevant to your industry. Mention why you like it.

People are curious. If you plant great conversation starters, they will take over. Once they ask, feel free to share. You'll figure out how to finesse these posts with practice. Just make sure that when you start, you are very mindful of the balance you are trying to keep.

To test the "lurkers" post a cryptic message about a great day or surprise coming up via your social sites. Then stay tuned online and in person to see who is paying attention. You may be surprised how many people see it online, don't like or comment, and ask you in person what you have coming up!

The Shiny Stuff – Keeping your Focus

Let's take a minute and address one of the key objections busy business people have with Facebook and social media sites in general. The main objection is that it can be a huge waste of time. It's important to understand the distraction potential when we get involved in social media.

It is fun. It's easy to connect with people who we have not seen in years and to look around with curiosity. We can spend countless hours just creating conversation, viewing interesting new things, even commenting on the photo albums of your old high school buddies. This is a good thing potentially for you personally, though it may not be the most productive time you can spend for your business; unless you take after the insurance agent who was able to leverage Facebook beautifully by becoming re-acquainted with the people in his sphere. It is critical to have a sound strategy in place so that you understand where your efforts should be focused and when you have time to be on your own relaxed time. It's essential that you know exactly what it is that you would like to accomplish and to stay on task. Don't go chasing after "the shiny stuff."

Of course, "the shiny stuff" can be a lot of fun. You can learn a great deal about new things. It can even be one of the best ways to make or reinforce your social connections – which can and do lead to business connections. When you are working within social media for your business, you set the strategy. Sometimes you find amazing things and new concepts, in "the shiny stuff" that you can leverage for your business. If you are limited on time and resources, however, don't let "the shiny stuff" distract you. If you are on focus, this is a huge tool, and there are incredible possibilities.

If you need that time to play with "the shiny stuff," set specific chunks of time aside.

Recognize this is your personal time and not part of your social media strategy. Set some time aside in the evening or whenever it is best for you, but while you are here for business, make it be for business. You can still have fun, just stay on task.

Social Relationships on LinkedIn

LinkedIn is the most professional of the social media sites available. LinkedIn originally was started as an online Rolodex, as a way to connect with your connections' connections. Say you have 10 business associates, and they each have 10 associates. LinkedIn was created as an easy platform from which to make introductions and expand your own network through referrals and personal recommendations.

Here's an example of the numbers with Sandi's account. She is connected to roughly 1,500 people in her first-level connections, meaning that she has requested to be linked to them or they agreed to be linked to her based on an existing relationship; they are a direct first level connection. Of those original 1,500 people, she requested to be connected with everyone in their first-level, about 515,000 people. So Sandi's sphere of influence of 1,500 just went to 515,000 plus her 1,500 original connections. LinkedIn takes this one level further, to a third-level connection. The third level is where the power of the tool becomes huge. In this example, the third level connections bring Sandi to 11 million additional people she can contact.

As LinkedIn is one of the most "professional" of the social media sites, there is not as much of your warm and fuzzy information on LinkedIn compared to Facebook. Typically, your LinkedIn profile is like an online resume, a digital story of your career and your professional background. When you are creating your LinkedIn profile, make sure that you include some "keywords" that relate to your career, so people can find you by what you do. For example, if you are a certified tax accountant, you want those words to appear in your work history, your educational experience and your groups, associates and interests. This helps other people find you by those words when searching LinkedIn.

Social Relationships on YouTube

When building your online presence, it would be a great idea to post a YouTube video on your site's home page. It can be simple—just introduce yourself, thank people for visiting your website, and give them a little taste of what they'll find. Your site visitors are there to interact and video is a great medium for this.

Tip: Allow your site visitors to click on the video to play it; instead of having the video start automatically. Auto-play can be annoying! If you take the alternative to let it start up without sound, it may just seem broken.

Update: Flash[33] is also on its way out of favor with websites, so really, don't be that auto play guy (or girl!)

In this new marketplace, we do business with people, not companies. Video is a great way to let prospects get to know you and the people in your company. Creating a video can be a relatively simple process. Using a digital camera, or your phone[34], it really is simple to capture, edit and upload clips for use online. As a general rule of thumb, keep an introductory video short. Typically, 30 to 90 seconds fits the attention span of most site visitors. If you are creating a how-to video or tutorial, it can be longer, but generally the shorter the better for info videos.

When creating video, please remember, just like your website is not about you, your video is not about you either. Your focus is on the person viewing the video and what you would like to share with them. Your job is to make it easy for them to get to know you, create a connection, and help reinforce your relationship. Videos are great for increasing the recall rate of who you are, what you do, and why we are visiting your

---

[33] A multimedia and software platform used for creating vector graphics, animation from the early 2000's

[34] We could have said smart phone, however, since you are reading this book we are making the assumption that you are smart, and have a smart and trendy newer phone. Well, new for 2015 anyway…

website. The more ways that we interact with visitors on our websites, the more traction we can create in their top of mind awareness. The more memorable we make ourselves, the more likely we are to be remembered when the next opportunity comes along.

One of our secrets of doing video for our pool company is that we share everything. We share thoughts and philosophies, how to and step by step instructions. By sharing everything we do, we are fun, relatable, knowledgeable, helpful, and memorable to our viewers. We are engaging and the feedback is fantastic!

Here is a little experiment: Next time when you are watching commercial television, ask yourself during the 2nd set of commercials "What Do I remember about the first set of commercials? Do I remember an emotion, a particular scene, a slogan, a person's face, and, dare I hope, maybe even the product or cause of the commercial? What made it effective?" If you really want to have fun, ask someone, who did not know that there would be a quiz, these questions.

If you find this intimidating at first, don't worry, just get your first video done and posted, and it will get easier each time. One of the beautiful things about video is its self-contained aspect. It is its own package, entirely. When someone else shares your message with their friends, there's no room for misinterpretation. They hear what you said and see what you showed. It is as simple as that.

Defining Your Certain Way

When you have clearly defined the center square of YOU, and become clear about your target audience, begin to think like them, you will be able to put messages in front of them that are exactly what they need to see. Your Energy Signature will become an even more important part of everything that you do, you will be able to make and utilize connections. Working on sharing your message with your social networks and building relationships will take your message even further.

Refer to the Appendix for even more suggestions and advice for beginning your connections via social channels.

Now onto the square where we get to be really creative, The Stuff!

The "Stuff"

{Middle, Right}

Just like the materials we use to build, our marketing resources can take on new life in other forms.

"Creativity is just connecting things. When you ask creative people how they did something, they feel a little guilty because they didn't really do it, they just saw something. It seemed obvious to them after a while. That's because they were able to connect experiences they've had and synthesize new things."
~ Steve Jobs

Those words of Steve Jobs ring so true for us. Our company is quickly earning a reputation for taking old things—stuff that many would consider junk—and repurposing them in a new way.

Take barn wood for example. In Al's travels around Michigan, he often comes across really old barns—100 or 200 years old—in danger of collapse. Al enjoys talking to the owners and seeing if they'd be willing to part with the wood. He makes it clear that he's not going to burn it or destroy it, but rather lovingly and respectfully incorporate that material into a new project. Give it a new life.

We do the same thing with our marketing. A video interview we post on YouTube is repurposed into a blog post. Then it might be expanded into a full length feature article that appears in an industry publication like *AQUA Magazine.* A collection of those articles might be turned into a book (*Our Certain Way*, 2015[35]) and voila, we have a cohesive and comprehensive marketing presence.

That's the beauty of repurposing your content, your original thoughts and ideas. As you get more comfortable with every channel, you'll begin to know what works best. You will see where and how to get the most out of every piece you create.

This square is about the *giveaway*, and the *leave behind*, the "*stuff*" that we have printed and produced to leave with various prospects out in the world. Some of the stuff we use for the pool company includes our portfolio books and our awesome sweatshirts. The portfolio books are used for a quick glance during our initial visit with a prospective homeowner. We leave them behind with the right homeowners, to be reviewed as the pool design process begins. (Or not, not everyone who gets a book gets a pool from us.) The sweatshirt, well people just love to wear it! [36] At the 2014 Atlantic City Pool Show our team showed up to a fancy steakhouse sporting our Pool Guys Sweatshirts, both with

---

[35] A great read as well!

[36] Just think, Al can see himself coming and going, especially at work and pool shows. And to answer your thought "I could never put my picture on a shirt!" Al had that thought too. He says he only has one face, so he might as well get used to it.

pride and hesitation as it was a bit of a nicer place. Shortly into the meal, the maître d, who happened to be bald himself remarked on how awesome he thought the sweatshirt was. We asked him for his address and size, and when he said what would fit him, Mark took the new sweatshirt he had been wearing off and promptly gave it to him. Photos and smiles ensued, and we had a story to share on social media, and great vibes of positive energy all around.

We've become known at the shows as "the sweatshirts"

We have witnessed a trend when a business decides to market. They often focus almost exclusively on their "stuff." The business owner, will decide to start their promotion for a product or service, and their very first activity is to figure out how to make a new brochure or other handout to give to people.

If you've been following along at all what might you have noticed about the order of the Organic Marketing™ process? How about the fact that we don't get to the "stuff" until we've worked through quite a few other squares in this process? Stuff can be highly effective, as long as it's the right stuff, for the right audience, with the right purpose.

The first step in determining how to create your stuff is to consider the purpose of the stuff. It is very important that all stuff have a reason for being. Don't just create it because you think you need it or you will be wasting time and energy. Most effective marketing materials have a clearly defined purpose. A brochure can be created to share information, create top of mind awareness, or result in an action being taken. A radio advertisement can do the same. As you begin to pay attention to marketing media, you'll notice in some cases there doesn't seem to be any real reason for the message you heard or saw. Understanding your purpose before you develop it will prevent this from happening to you.

An important key to sharing your Energy Signature is how it is represented in the stuff. This is where we express our persona and our personality, share our message, and inspire and influence those around us. This includes many of the activities that we have talked about to this point, connecting with people, working within our spheres of influence, and working within our social networks.

Energy Signature and your Relationships

The Energy Signature comes through in everything that we do online, in person, and through our stuff including our leave behinds, business cards, billboards, videos or sound bites. Our Energy Signature exists in thoughts about us and in the materials we produce. Any time that somebody thinks about us, our Energy Signature is engaged.

Leave-Behinds with a Purpose

There are incentive offers and then there's the "leave-behind." Think of the leave-behind as an item that is tangible. It is produced in hard form to leave in a prospect's hands or in their minds. These may include everything from print advertising, flyers, business cards, to your radio, television and billboard ads.

In designing your leave-behinds, think about why you are creating it and leaving it behind. Just leaving it because you are supposed to leave something is not a good enough reason to do it. It needs to serve a purpose. Have a specific goal in mind when you create it. What is the call to action? What do I want people to do when they get this leave-behind? What is your reason for making that piece?

The media selection you choose has a lot to do with the targeted reason for the piece. The results of a leave-behind or print advertisement need to be measurable. The goal is, when somebody has that piece, they are inclined to do something and you can measure the results. If you run an ad, is there a call to action? Is there a phone number that prompts people to call?

The purpose of a flyer might be advertising an upcoming event. Someone will get it, look at it, and then decide if this fits in their schedule or not.

The ideal action with a flyer promoting an event is that they will take the information and they will put it into their calendar, and in the best case pass it along to someone else. Informational pieces have a time and place, but if there is no call to action, it is hard to gauge how effective those really are.

Even your business card should have a purpose. Do you just want people to have your contact information? If you really want them to remember you, put your photo on your card. This is the #1, most effective element we have added to our business cards. People love it. We just wonder why so few people do this?

When you give someone your card do you want them to visit your website or maybe follow you on Twitter? Design that into your card and give the complete URL they can use to find you online. Understanding why you are leaving something behind is the best way to spend your money wisely when choosing media for a campaign.

These business cards were designed by Rebecca Osterman of Green Otter Graphics[37], and featured photos prominently. We encourage you to think about adding your photo to your business cards if it is not on there already. Just look at how much they stand out!

If you are doing any type of printed leave behinds, what do you suppose the most important aspect of it should be? Whether it's a card, a brochure, or a postcard, when someone looks at it they should be able to determine what to do next. Do you want them to visit your website to find out more about you? Would you like them to call for more information? Are they supposed to file it? Set an appointment? Fold it

---

[37] greenottergraphics.com

into a paper airplane and enter it in a contest? Here is another place that being highly visible with photos of you and your team is priceless. Again, not nearly enough people put their photos on everything!

A common result of "stuff" is getting people to visit your website. Once they arrive, you should also have a plan for what you want to happen next. In many cases, you want to try to capture their email address. By asking for their email address, in exchange for something that our visitor wants, they are essentially giving us permission to market to them in the future. In this exchange, we are offering them something of value – an e-book, a special offer, an incentive to get them to sign up to subscribe to our blog – something they find valuable enough to trade for their email address. Another result of visiting your website could be social sharing your site or your photos. Well placed social share buttons and links to your sites are great for additional promotion.

In developing online stuff with your incentives, ask yourself how you can engage people to do something with you, so that their visit to your site is an effective one and that it results in an inspired action. Some incentive ideas are informational documents, a download for a free book or industry insider report. The key is to make sure you are getting something of value from them (email address) and they feel they are getting something of value from you. As you move forward and develop your email marketing strategy, there will be more to consider to create a valuable exchange for both parties.

ABC Lists and Email Marketing

As you develop your Organic Marketing™ strategy you will begin to build a list which we refer to as your ABC's. [38]

As a refresher:

A's are people who know and love you. They talk about you to others, understand very well what it is that you do and who you are (they understand the center square of you).

Your B's are people that you may have recently met. They have probably heard of you and could, with some accuracy, talk about you. You may have become a recent Connection or had an interaction with you via your Social Relationship building.

Your C's are more distant "Universal" connections. They may have come across something you shared once or been introduced to you in passing. They don't know much about you, yet. The plan though, with your successful Organic Marketing™ presence, is that they will begin to bump into you and your message more often. They will gradually begin to move from

---

[38] This concept is also discussed earlier in this book in the Connections Square

your C list to your B list, and even possibly to your A list.

One way of marketing to a C or B list is by beginning an email drip campaign. Short information notes on a regular schedule. Maybe they found one of your videos on YouTube and subscribed. Maybe they were introduced to you and liked your Facebook page. A word of caution about email marketing: Once your visitor gives you an email address, don't start spamming them to sell, sell, and sell!

This is the time to slowly "drip" information to them:

- ✓ Tips & tricks about things you know that are related to your business
- ✓ Upcoming new products and/or services
- ✓ Events you have coming up
- ✓ Events you attended and something great you have to share with them
- ✓ Specific product improvements
- ✓ Significant staff changes (Significant to them!)
- ✓ ... And more that you can think up!

Give them a place to interact with you and make it worthwhile. Keep in mind WIIFM? (What's in it for me?) If you are just spamming them with information, they are going to run away. You may sell something every once in a while because you will catch someone in a buying cycle, but it is not going to be something that will build and sustain long-term relationships with your prospects. You must think long-term in this process. Make sure that you are capturing their email information and that you are trading something of value, in order to obtain this information and continue to use it time and time again.

Since our website is our favorite place for people to visit us, our stuff is created to reinforce our brand and not drive direct traffic. Some of our favorite stuff includes custom Monopoly™ games customized with our project photos, puzzles with our pools on them, coffee mugs and shot glasses, beach towels, t-shirts, sweatshirts, knit hats and baseball caps. We even have a Pool Guy Rubik's Cube[39] and Woolly Willy[40] magnet game!

Defining your Certain Way

When you have clearly defined your center square of YOU, and become clear about your target audience, begin to think like them, you will be able to put messages in front of them that make an impact. Begin to harness your Connections and Social Networks. Be super creative and have fun with your Stuff!

---

[39] Virtually impossible to solve

[40] Well, Woolly Pool Guy

Next we will begin to work with Strategic Alliances to continue to enhance your message and your reach.

Strategic Alliances

{Bottom, Middle}

Are you fostering relationships that will help you grow?

Attending Trade Shows and Creating Alliances

In the early days of my pool career, I worked for a builder here in Michigan. From the start I constantly wanted to learn more. I pored over the magazines that came through the office, devoured the few books I could find on the subject, and constantly bugged my boss about going to the trade shows.

He was more interested in keeping the status quo than in expanding his horizons, and the pool shows were just not on his radar screen.

It's not that he didn't learn about new products; he would talk to the sales reps who came by with the latest pump or new gadget, and if it looked like something that could make his life easier without having to adapt the way he did things, he would use it.

Meanwhile, I was always curious and wanting to be ahead of the curve, always imagining new solutions to the challenges faced in the field every day.

Several years later, after buying the company, we were struggling week to week just to keep our heads above water. At one point we owed a vendor a couple of thousand dollars, and the rep came into the office to collect. I had to tell him that he'd have to wait a few more weeks, because we were spending what little money we had to attend the pool show.

He was not happy. He couldn't see past the dollar signs and realize that by attending that show we were investing in the company and committed to growth, which would mean a bigger account for him too if he could stick with us.

His reaction was a revelation for me. This guy's shortsightedness represented a mindset of lack and want, and I realized he didn't have what it would take to grow with us. We paid him off, but did very little business with him after that. Looking back it was a pretty big mistake on his part.

Not going to trade shows is the same kind of mistake in my opinion. In my years in the business I've found three specific reasons to keep attending trade shows, even when money is tight or business is crazy busy.

Reason One: The Products

We did end up going to that event, and I saw a huge array of new stuff. Amazing stuff...products my sales reps never shared, and things I never dreamed existed. The immersion in new products and technology was intense. It was a huge investment in my own knowledge base, and worth the cost for that reason alone.

At another show several years ago, I came across a product that beautifully solved an ongoing problem we were having with our concrete slides. This was early on in the hybrid pool movement, and we didn't have a good solution for a finishing treatment.

We met a vendor using round penny tiles to surface a concrete slide. It was a wow moment for me, and I came home so excited. I took the crew back to six or seven previous jobs, stripped them down and used the penny tiles to resurface them. The customers were thrilled, and we were able to up our game and be ready for the next project.

Without speaking to this vendor face to face at the show, I never would have hit upon this particular solution. Industry shows give us the time to explore the off-book ideas or the "let's try this" moments that lead to breakthroughs.

Reason Two: The Relationships

In this industry, we walk that fine line between searching for the best price and getting the best perceived value. For me, it's important to build a supply chain I can rely on, so I can innovate and build with confidence.

One vendor we've worked with for years was Kafko Pool Products. We started using Kafko liners through a local supplier and loved the product. When our supplier closed we went direct to Kafko for our needs, building a good relationship with the folks in the manufacturing division.

When Latham came along and bought up the Kafko line, we were concerned that we'd be too small a fish for them to pay much attention to us. We needed this product; it was a crucial part of our supply chain.

By making a point to reach out the Latham execs at industry events, we were able to get them invested and excited in what we were doing, and create a solid relationship with them, both on a business and a personal level.

Reason Three: The Hidden Solutions

Every once in a while you learn something at a show that completely changes the way you approach your work.

At one event I heard a presenter[41] speaking about working with glass tile. He spoke about the science behind color theory[42], and my head started going a mile a minute. His ideas tapped into everything I had learned about art and design in school, and gave me an exact answer to all my questions about why color works the way it does. It has dramatically changed the way I approach color in my projects, and there's no way I would be this successful without that knowledge of color theory[v].

Sadly, I talk to a lot of pool guys in my local area who never go to the shows and see no reason to do so. And I hear those same folks grumbling that there's not enough business or too much competition in the industry.

To them I say "Get out there." Educate yourself, build relationships, get inspired.

It not only helps your own business, it also raises the entire industry to the next level. Let's work on our alliances and toward raising all of us up to the next level.

---

[41] Feras Irikat (A pool industry member)

[42] Specifically Robert Dorr's theory of color

Real Advice to Help You Define Your Niche

In our[43] mammoth $51 billion dollar a year industry[vi], defining your own niche can be a real challenge.

The first step is to decide what you want your niche to be, what you hope to accomplish with your marketing. For us, we had two major goals: 1) to set Legendary Escapes apart as a boutique custom pool company; and 2) to create a human voice and a solid presence in our industry and a position as experts in pool construction and service.

We had noticed that there wasn't any one person speaking as a resource for the industry— for pool builders, manufacturers, and homeowners. There was a real lack of a "go to" guy for these kinds of questions.

Our CMO Sandi Maki[44] was the brains behind the actual marketing plan to build our niche. We started to build a persona — "Ask the Pool Guy" —who was a source of information for manufacturers, suppliers, other pool builders and customers. We began posting informational videos on YouTube, blogging weekly, and engaging in social media in all kinds of pool and outdoor lifestyle discussions.

---

[43] Swimming Pool Construction and Service

[44] And fellow author of this book

We started going to the local and national pool conventions, filming videos and doing on-the-spot Q & A sessions, and talking to everyone we could meet in the industry. We had "Ask the Pool Guy" images plastered over everything—and I do mean everything: trucks, vans, pens, t-shirts, puzzles, coffee mugs, towels, blankets, boxer shorts, the crew's work gear, M & M's Candies, and of course all over social media.

We didn't have an end game at these events. We went to talk to people, share our ideas, give them a chance to talk about their business and share our passion for ours.

Before we knew it, the "Ask the Pool Guy" persona became a real presence both online and in real time, with people recognizing me and the crew as if they knew us. Because really, with our heavy social media and live network presence, they did, in many ways, know us already.

With this new found "celebrity" we were able to build Legendary Escapes into the boutique business we knew it should be—manned by a small crew of dedicated and talented people who are passionate about what we create and deliver. The more we engaged, the more our reputation grew and we are now in the fantastic position of being able to pick and choose the projects we take on each year.

We have the outrageous fortune to be able to work with people who understand our passion and feel the same. If our heart-felt approach to the craft doesn't make sense to someone, they're probably not our kind of customer. And that's okay! There are other pool companies that can meet their needs.

If I had to give you just one piece of advice, it's this: Just keep showing up. At industry events, at local networking events, on social media—show up to learn, to connect, to grow your knowledge base and increase your influence. Don't look for a specific return on investment for this time. It's not about how much you sell at a particular event, or how many business cards you collect. It's about all the folks you meet, the knowledge you offer, and engaging with the influential people in your industry.

It's in these things that your niche comes to life and is the fastest way to creating and strengthening your alliances.

Creating Alliances

Strategic alliances are associations that you have with other people, organizations and businesses. Creating strategic alliances is one of the best things that you can do for your business. Some of the best alliances can be with people within your industry. With the strategic alliance approach, we really need to retrain ourselves in thinking that everybody is a collaborative and potential creative resource for us. In this new human-based economy, we are all collaborators.

If you are looking to create alliances with other people and businesses in your industry, you need to look on a broad scale and recognize there are enough clients for everyone. Don't be afraid to talk to those people who once were your "competition." It doesn't apply now. Build relationships with them. Share information with them. Co-sponsor a webinar together. Invite them to guest author a piece in your next newsletter or guest post in your blog. The key is to think outside the traditional scope of business. You can have alliances with people who do the exact same thing you do because you are going to have different specialties and different Energy Signatures. These alliances broaden your sphere of influence and build your credibility.

Another avenue to create alliances is with suppliers and wholesalers. Begin to think of and go to them with creative ideas on how you can work together. That is a huge piece of the equation. Your wholesale contacts want you to succeed because your success breeds their success. If you are purchasing from them, you are selling their products. They should likely want to help you succeed. You might not go to your supplier because you think, "Well, we are just one little fish in a big pond." Stop thinking that way. Build relationships there and co-promote products and how they work within your service offerings. You might even find that you are a big fish in one of their departments.

When you are looking for strategic alliances, think about your target customer. Who are they? What is their personality? What is the age demographic? You will be able to find another company that is talking to the same end user you want to reach, although you may think you have absolutely nothing in common. Brainstorm some creative ways to make connections with people who are serving the same audience. Consider making connections with people who have similar messages to yours, so you can share your marketing resources. You can share your information; you can promote each other back and forth. When you do this right, everybody wins. We have included handymen and landscaping promo items with our pool mailings for the price of shared postage. Get creative!

Alliances and Social Media

One of the things that really leverages the time we spend in social media is the ability to work with our strategic alliances. If your target demographic which you identified in square number three is, for example, age 35- to 45-year-old women; find someone else who has that same demographic target. Then create marketing messages that you both share on your pages, promoting each other. This can be in a totally different industry, yet you can share your people with them and they can share their people with you.

We get so involved with our own stuff; we think our message is clear and compelling.[45] Yet we really need someone else to look at it and say,

---

[45] No need to say brilliant, of course.

"Are you sure that is what you are trying to say?" Because it is not what you say; *it is what people hear*. Having a sounding board, a guide, or a coach will be invaluable to help guide you through the process of clarifying your message, and sharing it with others, will make a big difference.

One last task in the Alliances Square is to find someone who can filter information for you. In the social media realm, so many things are happening that you cannot possibly keep track of it all, but there are plenty of filters available. There are people who spend a lot of time at this. At the InSights Community, we have become a filter to many of our community members, much like our mentors are filters who pass information onto us. Create some filters of your own so you are not out there chasing it all by yourself.

Defining Your Certain Way

When you have clearly defined your center square of YOU, and become clear about your target audience, begin to think like them, you will be able to put messages in front of them that are speaking directly to them! Begin to harness your Connections and Social Networks. Make sure you think through your Stuff, and begin to work with Strategic Alliances to continue to enhance your message and your reach.

Next, is where we tie this all together. We'll move into your Online Home that becomes the foundation for your entire marketing presence.

Your Online House

{Bottom, Right}

How to build a solid brand in the connection economy

"Be genuine.
Be remarkable.
Be worth connecting with." —*Seth Godin*

In the old-school "transactional selling" model, there's no relationship past the immediate purchase. In the pool business, maybe they remember you and call you back next season or maybe they call the guys down the road. It makes no difference to them; your business is just one of many and the bottom line is generally price or availability.

What would it mean to your business if customers sought you out, instead of the other way around? What if people called you because they heard about you from a friend or saw your post on Facebook? In our own experience as owners of Legendary Escapes, it changes everything.

We started building an online presence around 2007, connecting with customers, friends and prospects and building great relationships with folks online. We based it on a friendly "Pool Guy" character and started publishing content with the theme of "Ask the Pool Guy."

How to Find and Tap into Your Local High End Niche

So many of us start out in this business of building pools for the mass market; basic designs for basic budgets, nothing really special or unique, but there are plenty of customers to buy what we are building. If volume is your thing, then this might be a business model that makes good sense.

For us, this wasn't the kind of business we wanted. Rather than quantity, we were hungry for creativity. We didn't care so much about how many pools we built; we just wanted each of them to be truly unique. And we wanted to do it locally, staying in southeast Michigan while we grew.

Crazy? Maybe, but it's not the first time I've been accused of that (and probably not the last).

Granted, Michigan is not the first place you think of as a hot spot for the pool industry. Between the tough climate (we have just a few good months of pool weather every year) and the economy (Michigan is always among the first to feel the pinch, and the last to recover) we've got our share of challenges.

And we did it anyway.

In thinking back on how we did it, how we built a high-end artistic hybrid pool company by tapping our local market, I realized there were three major turning points for us along the way.

Famous for What?

I spent a lot of time researching and paying attention to builders that were known for original, creative projects instead of building standard, basic-budget pools. I studied the types of projects they built, the materials they were using, and the ways they were putting their projects together. I became really good at identifying each local builder by their individual style. From this knowledge I envisioned the kinds of pools I would build when I had the budgets they were working with. In other words, I started to define what I'd be known for – completely custom artistic hybrid pools.

I realized, as I studied the companies that I admired that were doing this, that they were dealing with an entirely different type of clientele.

They certainly weren't the kind of client I was used to having, with set budgets and set expectations as to what a "pool" means. So I asked myself, "How can I find a client who is willing to hire me to do this different thing I want to try?"

As I talked to more and more prospects, I found a very receptive audience when I suggest a new idea or an unusual design. The key was in having a clear idea of the kinds of pools I wanted to build, and asking my clients to let me do it. Once I could articulate my vision, they began to say yes.

How Much are You Worth?

I've shared this story before, about my customer who was so pleased with the final results that he told me flat out I could have charged 50% more for the project and he would have happily cut me a check. This blew me away, as I began to realize that not only were my skills and craft advancing with each project, my value was going up accordingly.

People were not just buying my pool building skills; they were not buying the concrete and the boulders and the rock and the tile. They were buying my art and my creativity, the part of my business that feeds my soul and keeps me slogging through the concrete day after day.

Sure, there were some new things we tried that we didn't make a ton of money on. But we never gave our work away, like some folks in the industry recommend. Once you realize what you are worth, you can charge accordingly without hesitation. This is a critical step in finding clients with those dream budgets. They don't expect you to work for cheap; they expect to pay for the skills you bring to the project.

Tell the Right Story

What we quickly realized is our ideal customer is not looking for a pool, they are hoping to create a lifestyle experience in their backyard. To provide that, we have to know why they are spending that kind of money, and understand what they expect to get out it.

They weren't doing it to impress their neighbors, or improve their property value. They were doing it to create an experience that suited their family, something specifically and uniquely their own.

Once we knew this, we could market to this audience using messaging that would resonate. We knew we were only going to get a very small percentage of the local pool buying market—and we were totally okay with that. We now had a voice and story to share that would resonate with the right clients, the ones who were looking for what we had to offer.

Social media and online marketing was the perfect vehicle for our marketing, as we were able to tap into an audience that was really receptive to what we had to say.

Ultimately, it was this process—defining what we wanted to do; understanding the value of what we offer; and telling the right story to the right people on our website and via social media—that got us out of that basic "starter pool" mentality and helped us create a thriving niche business that we love.

If you aren't building an authoritative presence online, where customers and prospects can find you, connect with you, and begin to build a relationship with you, you are stuck in a transactional economy where price becomes the determining factor and brand loyalty is nonexistent. And that is a very shallow pool.

The Foundation of your Online House

Square Nine is where Organic Marketing™ all comes together and it's centered on building a foundation with our online house.

In most cases, your online house will be your website, which should also house your blog. WordPress is a great platform to build your site in, as it will give you the blog capabilities that you need, and be relatively easy to access and maintain. The blog is the most important element because with it you can automate your content to your social sites, and the search engines love new and fresh content of blogs that are updated regularly.

A well designed website with a blog feature will be one of the best ways someone can get to know you. They might first learn from you, and then as they spend more time on your site they can get to know you and your brand based on the stories you tell and the information you provide.

When designing your site, keep the user experience in mind as the most important aspect of your site's development. Many people like to think about their website from their own perspective. Yes, you need to include things that you like, though it is most important to design the site for your users to enjoy, and to be able to quickly find what they are looking for. When you find the right blend of these elements, you will have a strong site and encourage the engagement and activity that you will benefit from.

A website should be informational, inspirational, educational (about you, your product or service), and should show your visitors how they can work with you. Your blog is the perfect place for you to begin to experience the shift we are seeing online today: trading knowledge for money.

If you are at the point where you are just getting a website started, you can start by writing your story, a little bit of it every day via

170

your blog posts. You may be surprised to find out that many of your existing contacts may not know or understand what you do, and as you start to share, they will begin to take notice and ask questions.

Your visitors at first may be friends and family. As you keep building your site, and building your blogging presence, as long as you are including relevant keywords, you will begin to build your global audience based on your area of expertise.

You will be amazed at the results that you will begin to see based on putting a few simple methods into practice. On your blog, share your ideas, your opinions, and education. Develop your site as the place where your visitors can come to receive your information and your insights.

As your site begins to gain traction, it is a great idea to add an email sign-up form on your blog, so readers who are interested can sign up for your newsletter, blog updates, and special messages.

All Roads Lead to your Online House

A funnel is an important aspect of your online house. If you've spent time and effort engaging in all of the areas we have covered so far in Marketing Tic-Tac-Toe, the next step when people get to your site is going to be funnel them through your information to where you'd like them to go.

In our Legendary Escapes[46] website we have thought through our funnel. We want visitors to find us online, and then discover our website. It is the main place that people will get to know us, so we feature photos of our projects. We also feature videos embedded on the site from YouTube, so visitors can begin to hear our stories first hand, and decide if they'd like to know more. We have addressed many of our frequently asked questions on our site, with pages dedicated to the questions of budget, and how to get started. We also have clear indications of the next step, which is typically calling the office to have a discussion about setting up an appointment. Our website has so much information on it that once someone begins to watch our videos and look through our galleries, they will begin to understand our philosophy and the culture of our company. We go as far as giving options for people if they discover they might not be a good fit for us, or if they are looking for something different than what we provide.

We have spent massive amounts of time on creating our funnel, and thinking through how to logically move people through the steps of learning about us, deciding if they'd like to work with us or get to know us better, to doing business with us, and then sharing us with

---

[46] www.legendaryescapes.com

others. Our website is the most important place for our consumers. It is also a work in progress, and because of the blog element something that we strive to update almost daily.

Once you have a well designed website, and are committed to blogging, you can begin to add additional elements like email marketing, affiliate marketing, events and well placed banners and ads.

You will also be able to point people to your online house from online and offline. As you meet people or they begin to know you, remember that all roads lead home. Every interaction you have online should have a findable link to your website. If you are attending in person networking events, or carrying business cards, everything you create should point to and support your online house.

At one time[47], the only way people could find out about you was to look you up in the Yellow Pages or ask a friend for a recommendation and give you a call. Thanks to technology, people are able to self educate about anything they are interested in. The first place most people turn is to the smart phone in their hand to initiate their search or quest for companies and information. By going through the process we have outlined in Organic Marketing, and in spending time

---

[47] As recent as when Al took over the pool business, and for a decade into his pool career...

developing each of your Marketing Tic-Tac-Toe squares, you'll be findable and connectable as soon as they start looking!

Since it will be so easy for people to find you, make it even easier on them. Your name should be a prominent part of all of your marketing, and it should be easy to find on your website. People are more likely to remember your name than a company name. When choosing your company name, if you happen to be that early in your business development, choose carefully. Something simple and catchy that easily translates into a website is a great direction to head. When you are choosing your website domain name, keep it simple, easy to spell, and memorable. When choosing, go with .com whenever possible as it is the first and most recognizable domain name. Think through what will represent you and your brand well, as well as lend credibility and fun energy to your efforts.

What Makes a Website a Destination?

Your website will be a destination if it has the information that people need, and elements that people like. As you are getting started, working with your strategic alliances will be a great way to gain some initial traction. You can easily interview your alliances and create blog posts and video talking about things you have in common. You would think this is more common (especially in the pool industry), and you may be surprised at how many people don't take the effort to interview vendors and talk about products with others to post on the website. We gain visibility, keywords, and visitors when we include links and stories about others in the industry on our site. We have also found that by sharing information that all pool users can find helpful that we are a go to resource for questions relating to swimming pools around the world. Many of our clients that live nearby and choose to work with us often cite our online presence, knowledge and willingness to help educate others as reasons that they chose to work with us.

Consistency is the key for your online house. It should be updated regularly, and in your voice following your energy signature. Many people are intimidated by the amount of work they think a website will take to develop—and they are right, it does take work to get started. Don't try to move the mountain all at once, take it one day, and one blog post at a time. Try to limit shortcuts. Sure, it is great to ask for help. Make sure when you do that your energy signature and your voice are present. People will be able to tell when you've hired the auto blogger to write those robotic posts or replies for you.

Keep your site active and fresh. Make your online house easy to find, recognizable in look and feel, and feature photos of you and your team prominently so people know when they are on your site so they will accept no substitutions! The elements of your Energy Signature are easily added to your site through photos, the vibe of the design of your site, and we always recommend a welcome video or two on the home page so people can get to know you quickly!

A few of the things that are the most engaging on a website include video, photos, interactive widgets, audio clips, and the ability to interact with you by leaving comments on blog posts and other content.

You will want to revise your website often. This is not a one and done task. It is something that you should design and develop, and continually improve and change.

Look at your current website. Consult with a website designer, and talk to somebody about website usability, to help you understand the experience from *the user's point of view*. Many businesses haven't actually taken the time to figure out who their site visitor is likely to be, and what features they would be looking for. Look at your website while thinking like your customer to make this concept come to life.

The key to great visits to your website comes down to the user experience. Add features to your website that your audience is looking for. Make sure that they are engaged when they get to your site, they can find what they are looking for, and they are guided through your funnel process to take an action before they leave. Most importantly, make sure your Energy Signature is well represented, and you and your team are showing up prominently!

Just because you love something does not mean your client feels the same way. If you love certain colors, or if you love Excel spreadsheets, you really should step back from your website and consider your user.

Evaluate the amount of time it takes to navigate to certain areas of your site. How intuitive is it? Consider if your user has a lot of time. Do they want to read a lot of technical information? Are they somebody who would like to click a lot of buttons? Do they enjoy the shiny stuff? Are they just looking for a quick answer? Would they like to see pictures of you, read stories about different things that are going on with your business and with your life?

Keep those things in mind, and your customers will have a unique and enjoyable website experience.

Your Digital Profile

Behind your blog and website, your digital profile is the larger online house, your sum total of everything you post online. Social media is a huge way for you to increase your digital profile. Your digital profile is the primary contact that you have with consumers worldwide. Think about those consumers looking for a product or service. Where are they going to go first? Chances are they are going to either ask a friend or do an online search. Statistically most of us go to Google.

All of the different social media sites you participate with help to build up your Google rankings. This is without paying a dime for search engine optimization (SEO). Through your social media connections, through your profiles, and the keywords that you use on your blog posts and in your site, you can increase the chances that your listing will come up near the top of a Google search for your key words.

We recommend that you do a Google search for your name and your company name. Find out what sites come up near the top of the list for you. Social media sites generally rank pretty well, so don't be surprised to find your Facebook Page listed in the top 10. Make sure that you have complete profiles and good information on the sites that come up near the top of the list. As you have time to dedicate to them, keep going down the list, expanding your online empire for the strongest online footprint possible.

Google and the other search engines[48] available are in the business of making recommendations and making referrals. If your name or your business doesn't come up on the first page of Google, it is like running a business with an unlisted phone number. With social

---

[48] Which we don't mention here because Google is really the biggest as of 2015. If you develop your site to show up well in Google, it will show up well in the other search engines as well.

media, the more profiles that you put up out there and the more active you are, the more relevant you become in the eyes of Google and more likely to be recommended; therefore, everything we mention doing is important for you to be found!

Email Signatures

You can also leverage your social presence, and get people to your website and social media sites, by effectively using your email signature.

Make it quick and easy for people to find you and connect with you online and off. If you are emailing someone, provide that easy way for them to learn more about you. You'd be amazed at how effective your photo will be for someone to get to know you (and recognize you in person) before you've even met!

Al often shares a story of when he and Sandi were speaking at an event on the west side of Michigan. They hadn't met their contact in person yet, but as soon as Sandi walked into the venue their contact recognized her, came right over and made the introductions! This was simply by just being recognized from her photo on her email signature. Use the options available in your email program to create a personalized signature on your email. Our recommendation is to keep it simple. Say who you are, share your photo, a social link or two and your website will be more than enough for someone to have more options to connect with you. Get creative and change things as well, if people become accustomed to always seeing the same thing, they are less likely to notice what you share. One week feature your Facebook page, and maybe the next you ask for a follow on Twitter. You'll know what the best options for you are, especially as you work through Tic-Tac-Toe and work on your strategies.

Your Blog, the Keystone of your Online House

One of the major benefits to blogging is that the search engines will get used to seeing new content on your website every day, so they will become conditioned to sweeping through your site on a regular basis to see what's new. Another benefit is that you will begin to gain some keyword rankings, if your blog is centered on a specific topic. This becomes very important when people are trying to find you online.

When you blog, you may be tempted to start a blog on a free website, wordpress.com or blogspot.com. We recommend that you own your real estate online, by purchasing a domain name and running a self-hosted WordPress blog. Typically, a hosting service[49] will have a one click installation for your WordPress blog, so the initial setup isn't that challenging. You may want to bring in a web developer to help walk you

---

[49] We suggest Bluehost.com.

through some of the set up and customization, depending on how much time, effort and energy you want to put into the process.

There is a lot to be considered when you are putting together your blogging strategy. Clarify your goals, the method that you will use to share your message, and how you best package it to put it in front of people so that they feel compelled to share it with others and take an action as a result of having seen something that you have posted, written, or recorded. [50]

How Often to Blog

We recommend that you blog every day. If that's not possible, then aim for at least several times a week. Remember, the more frequent the posting, the more the search engines will visit your site, and your content will have a better chance of appearing in searches.

WordPress makes it simple to time-release your blog posts; if you have a block of time, you can write several new posts in one sitting and then schedule them to publish a new one once a day for a week or two. This is a great strategy if you plan to travel or have busy times at work when you can't spend time blogging. Not

---

[50] If you have been reading this book from the beginning, this may sound very familiar. Keep reading, there is more...

everyone is a writer. No problem. You can also hire some great content writers to share your message. You will want to work closely with someone who can communicate in the voice of your company, so that you are well represented online. You can also video blog—maybe you would prefer not to write and are comfortable in front of a camera. This can be very effective as well—just make sure it's worked in as a part of your overall strategy.

When we start a blogging strategy with someone, we often choose several topics of interest they would like to blog about. We set a theme for each day of the week. This helps clarify what to write about each time you begin to write a post. If we just sat you in front of a computer and said now blog, chances are your mind would go blank immediately. Instead, we suggest you frame your topics so that you know every Monday you are talking to a certain audience about a certain topic; this lets you pull your content together much more easily. Eventually, you may deviate from your original plan, and that's okay. The more comfortable you become with blogging, the more likely you will get to try new things.

What to Blog

The content strategy on a blog is really one of the most critical parts. The site needs to be interesting, at a glance, to your reader. Typically, a new visitor will spend just seconds on the site to determine if they are in the right place and if they can find what they need. The argument can be made for a blog site versus an older "static" type of website that once someone visits a static website, what compelling reason is there for them to go back? When you have a website that is structured as a blog, it is an indicator to people that there will always be something new, something fresh, and a reason to come back to read more.

When creating your content, consider:

Attractive—your blog posts need to be interesting and engaging to the reader. Your visitors are not robots; they need stories and things to keep their attention.

Keywords—identify a few key phrases that someone might type into Google, for example, to find your service or information on the topic you are blogging about. These keywords should be included in your posts, but not obviously. They should flow with the theme of your posts.

Clear—Readability is important. Blog posts should be relatively short. A reader will land on a page and spend only seconds deciding if they are interested in the information. A couple of paragraphs, often with bullet points or a numbered list, will help the reader get to the information that they need quickly.

Blog posts can host a variety of content. You can have written posts, photos, audio, video or any combination of the above. When you are writing blog posts, we recommend you add a photo to the post because it gives the eye somewhere to land on your page and immediately engage. This is important for allowing just a moment for comprehension to set in, it also showcases your posts very well via social sharing sites like Facebook.[51]

Think about why you want to start your blog. Start it because you have something to say and you have a message that you would like to share with the world.

Start a blog because you have social media sites, like Facebook, LinkedIn, and Twitter, and you would like to have relevant information posting to them on a regular schedule. If you decide you would like to try blogging and are planning to only post once a month or so, blogging is probably not right for you. People visit your blog to read new information, fresh information, ideally every day.

For your blog to truly become a resource, people must know that they can stop in tomorrow and they will find something new,

---

[51] And, certainly a picture is still worth a thousand words.

unique, and interesting. A goal of a good blog is to be so effective in the message that you share, that people want to get updates on your content, in some cases every day, by subscribing to your RSS feed. RSS stands for "really simple syndication," and is a way for a reader to subscribe to the content on your blog and have it delivered either to their email inbox or their preferred blog reader.

Getting the ideas for blog posts comes from many different sources. Start within your industry and do research. Find out what some of the trending topics are and what people are talking about. Look at the blogs that you follow—how are those authors creating content that is interesting and what keeps you coming back? Post your opinion, as comments, on some of the posts that you read on other blogs. Become engaged in conversation. Share helpful links to other sources of information. Your opinion may include why you find it a helpful resource—or not. Add your thoughts about what sparked in your creative consciousness.

You can also review products and services that would be of interest to your readers. Share this as a resource you have found that you think your readers may find helpful. Keep your post informative. Make your readers aware of various events, industry happenings, and news of interest. After you have been blogging for a while, look back on some of your blog posts. Is there information that you could update, that you could make new again by adding a new opinion or another element? Look at what you have written about, and expand on that information in new posts.

Blog Content Tips

- ✓ Use short headlines that will entice your readers to click to get the rest of the story.
- ✓ The first sentence of your post is critical. It's what people will see when you automate your posts to publish on your various social media sites. Make it compelling.
- ✓ Tell a story in your post, with relevant keywords.
- ✓ People like quick bullet pointed lists; it makes the content easier to skim.
- ✓ Be positive and inspiring. That gets huge response and share rates.
- ✓ If you have a new post, share with the words: "new post" or "this just in" or "wonderful news" to let people know that it's not something they've seen before.
- ✓ Share at the times of day when your audience is likely to see your content. Early morning, evenings and weekends can be good, but your audience might have their own trends.
- ✓ Share appropriate content at appropriate times. Business news early is best shared early in the business day; inspiration and entertainment in the evenings and weekends.

- ✓ Inspire, inform, educate and repeat.
- ✓ If you want comments on your post, ask for them. If you don't ask, we don't answer.

Blogging Strategy

Let's take a minute to develop your personalized blogging strategy. Start with your website. Figure out the best way to incorporate a blog into your site. Maybe the site that you are using has an application that you can add to start blogging. If you're not sure, talk to your web designer to see if incorporating a WordPress blogging platform makes sense for you. Whichever way you do it, once you start writing your first post, make sure that you have an attention-getting headline. Make it interesting.

When you get into the body of your post, keep it short. Two paragraphs is a great length. The idea is to inform quickly and get immediate reads. If you end up writing a post and it turns into three, four, and five paragraphs, you have probably got enough information to do a series of posts, to be released one day after the other. Don't try to cram a lot of content into a single blog post unless it is ultra time sensitive. Let the story continue by asking the readers what they thought. Have them share their story. Ask for feedback. Make sure that, when you have asked for feedback from your readers, you revisit your blog to comment back. Once they have made a comment to you, make this a two-way conversation. Blogging is all about conversation, so make sure that you are reading what your readers (and audio/video listeners) have to say.

Blog programs have an on/off switch to allow readers to post comments. Allowing comments is one of the scariest parts for people who are not currently blogging. What if someone says something unfavorable? What if someone becomes controversial or belligerent?

Realize that you, as the blogger, can control what comments are made live. Now granted, this isn't all about you and about having it all show favorably to you; that is not its purpose. If comments come back that are not favorable to you, but they engage people into conversation, it is okay to be a little bit transparent and vulnerable. Recognize that it is a growth opportunity when you can engage people to talk about whatever the subject is. Discuss their different opinions. Just don't get nasty or snarky...you'll lose more than one reader if you do that.

There are enough controls built into most blogging platforms to allow you to monitor, ban users if necessary, and be able to put your best foot forward for your company and for your blog site.

Increase your engagement by taking the link for your blog and posting it in specific places. If you have answered a question that was covered well on another blog, you can link over to that posted answer, as an additional resource. This is also a great thing to do with other people's blogs that you find interesting.

Share other people's information. Post about them on Facebook. Share it with a Twitter post. Make sure that you are letting the world know about the posts and blogs that you find interesting and relevant.

Another way of gaining readership is to ask people to review your posts as they go live. Simply ask the question, "Would you mind reading this and then tell me what you think?" As long as you are open and willing to listen to the opinions of what people have to say, you will find people who will follow your blog and read your posts. Ask your friends and your family. Ask your colleagues and people closest to you what they think about your blog. Is it interesting? Ask key people in your target audience what they would like to read about. If you do that, you will find that you have a lot of content, you have a lot of possibility, plus you have a lot of resources to go to when you are looking for inspiration. There are a lot of people who are willing to help. You might even learn that your top priority for improvements is way down on your client's list.

Defining Your Certain Way

When you have clearly defined your center square of YOU, and become clear about your target audience, begin to think like them, you will be able to put messages in front of them that they want to see, lead them to your online house!

You have begun to harness your Connections and Social Networks. You've thought through your Stuff, and have begun to work with Strategic Alliances to continue to enhance your message and your reach. Finally, you've brought it all together in your Online Home that will become the foundation for your entire marketing presence.

Congratulations, for making it this far!

Playing Tic-Tac-Toe

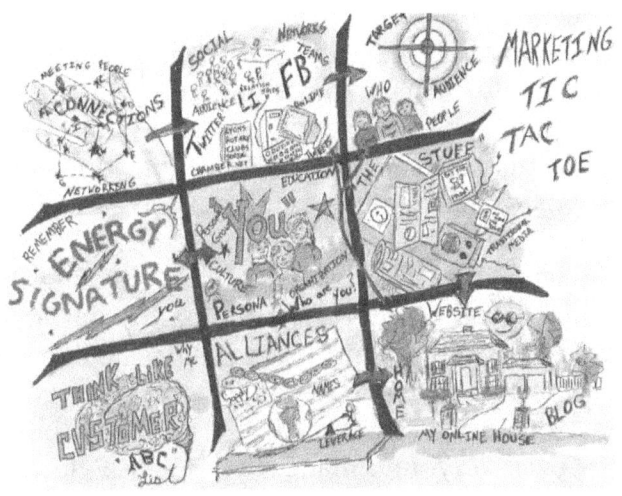

To recap Organic Marketing™ and the use of the Marketing Tic-Tac-Toe™ board, the element of YOU is the most important. YOU are the center square.

Focus on that center square all the time and be the student of that center square. This process is organic, which means that it is continually changing and growing. Personal growth and business growth both center on you.

As you focus on your center square, begin to define your target audience. Even more importantly, begin to think like them.

Think Like your Customer to build your tribe, by creating your ABC list and working continually to create successful top of mind awareness.

Create and define your Energy Signature—the definable "thing" you leave behind wherever you are, either in person or online.

Start to get involved in with your connections. Become more present in your social networks and building relationships and top of mind awareness through your interactions.

Then, look at the "stuff," all the different media—print copy, ads, billboards, business cards, CDs, sweatshirts, key chains and other types of creative items—and the message they leave behind.

Leverage your Alliances with those close to you, within your industry. Consider anyone who can help you and you can help in return.

Last, but not least, create a strategic online presence, with a website that is full of your Energy Signature, efficient in its arrangement of your information, and one that transitions people into purchasing from you. If your site is well organized, your customer should be able to quickly find what they need, learn more about you, and be able to make a decision about what their next step is with YOU.

This organic approach to marketing allows you to flow, it allows things to change, it allows you to look at your overall strategy day to day and be able to adjust it as you need to in order to move forward in the future and create all the success that you are looking for.

As you get more comfortable with the idea of the tic-tac-toe concept, you'll start to see new ways to connect, new places to strengthen your online persona and build your list.

You'll begin to see new ways to engage and build those online relationships. The main thing is to get started by looking at the squares, in the order we have spelled out in this book.

Just get started, and you'll be building your marketing strategy in an organic and authentic way.

Appendix:

Case Studies and Organic Marketing™ Examples

How Important is your Online Home?

We recently performed an Organic Marketing™ Review for a client using our tic-tac-toe board. The company was considering taking on a partner product line and even considering a complete re-brand. Part of their arrangement was to add their name to the other company, abandon their domain, and direct all their traffic to the new site. In exchange for this redirection and assimilation by their nationally-recognized partner, the new partner would provide any leads that come into this company's territory, for a price of $100 each.

As we progressed through the review, we came to the website and online house square. A quick peek at Google Analytics for the site showed well over 1,000 hits per month on this domain. At least 450 were generated in Michigan, where the company is located. We encouraged the company to keep their domain and not to redirect traffic to the national site. We even suggested that they sell leads to the national site, since the site was getting decent traffic for a specialty niche product.

We did the math. By keeping their domain to themselves, they are going to keep the traffic that is already coming in because of previous marketing. Any leads that come through the national site, they are willing to pay for. At a promise of three leads per week @$100/lead, we're talking an average of $1200/month. Multiply that by 12 and you've got $14,400. Just think what would have happened if they had redirected all their traffic and had to buy back all the leads coming from their site, still averaging over 1000 hits. They could have ended up buying what they already worked for on their own!

The Organic Marketing™ Review was relatively inexpensive and saved the company from making a big mistake. It pays to look at your entire marketing process when making decisions for online marketing, including social media and websites.

FREE HUGS – An Energy Signature Story

Allan: Sandi has a compelling story about how Free Hugs became an integral part of the InSights Community. She is somewhat reluctant to share the story, but with a little convincing, she has agreed to share it with you here.

Sandi: I would love to talk about *Free Hugs*[52], which has been so instrumental in my life, my professional growth, and in my speaking career. The *Free Hugs* concept came about as I was growing and changing with the InSights Community. I was growing and changing personally. With the concepts and the ideas that we had been masterminding at InSights, I was going through a lot of changing and a lot of growing, appreciating the small things.

---

[52] Once Sandi agrees to something, her energy signature supports it 100%.

Through this growth, I was reflecting on my childhood and growing up as the oldest of five children, the four others being my younger brothers. Our childhood was typical and I do remember in my elementary years being a bit of a tomboy. Once I got to high school, of course like any normal teenager, I spent less and less time at home. After graduation, and being the first out of the house, I lived out of state and moved around for a number of years. I missed many family holidays in the years after high school. As I became more established as an adult, I was able to make the return trips home. I'll fast forward to where the story picks back up.

The same year we opened InSights, I took my children back home to my parents' house to celebrate the holidays. My goal? To be more of a "big sister" to my brothers than I had been. Since my teenage years, we hadn't been all that close or warm and fuzzy. I decided (in line with my new active persona and Energy Signature) that it was time to make a huge deal out of reconnecting with my brothers. During this particular trip home, any time one of my brothers came into the room or left a room, I would jump up and run over and give them a big hug, making a huge deal out of the fact that I was getting to see them.

My kids, who were about 8 and 10 at the time, were watching this and looking at me like I was a little bit crazy. My brothers were not quite sure what was going on with their crazy sister. I kept this up throughout the holiday and, at the end of a visit with more hugs than normal, I headed back home. Nothing was really said about the experience by my brothers and I wonder if they were just a little bit relieved that the extra attention was gone.

A couple weeks later, I opened my email to find that one of my brothers emailed me a link to a YouTube video. There was no accompanying message, nothing saying, "I thought of you today." It was just a simple link. The link was to the *Free Hugs* campaign in California. There were people standing on the street corners with their signs, giving away *Free Hugs* and recording the footage so that they could share it with the rest of the world.

Well, that was the day that my markers came out and I created my own *Free Hugs* sign. I decided that I would start carrying the sign around the office and we would see what kind of culture change it might create. I didn't necessarily want to carry that sign with me every day (it sometimes seemed like work), but somehow I did for the first couple of weeks. Things began to change and the reactions to holding the sign were priceless. After that, even if I didn't bring the sign with me, people asked where it was. They wondered why we were not starting out the meeting with a hug. It started a change of the culture here at the InSights Community, thanks to that message from my brother.

My speaking career and the ability to get up in front of people and spontaneously deliver a message can also be attributed to the *Free Hugs* story.

We had been hosting a group that was aspiring public speakers. They would come into the InSights Community to practice, everyone would give a short speech and then the rest of the members would give suggestions on ways to improve. My mission was to be supportive and sometimes lead discussions, but not necessarily get up and give a keynote presentation. That was really Al's role as the "Orator."

I had shown up on a Saturday morning, to one of the public speaking meetings, and I was asked, "Would you like to give a speech?" I figured, sure, why not. I am always up for something new and I had no idea what I would talk about. I had about 5 minutes before it was time for me to get up, so I started thinking, "What can I talk about ... what can I talk about?" I looked over at my office, and it dawned on me ... *Free Hugs*!

I walked over and I picked up my sign, and they called me up to the front of the room. I still have the copy of that very first speech, where I spoke for 8 minutes extemporaneously on the story of *Free Hugs* and how they had come to the InSights Community.

When I was done speaking, of course, I was a little bit insecure. It was not a prepared speech and I was not sure how I did. These were people who participate in the public speaking world to a caliber that I haven't even aspired to. And they were giving me feedback, like it was excellent.

They couldn't believe that I had never given a speech before. One of them even said the speech should be made into a children's book!

That experience launched my confidence and my ability to command the presence in front of the room. From that day on, to enhance the culture of organizations that we were participating in, Al and I would often bring *Free Hugs* signs with us, whether it was an outside networking event or somewhere that we were brought in to speak about social media or business. Those *Free Hugs* signs were a great conversation starter and they were a great relationship builder. We have met so many amazing and supportive people, simply because we carried those signs with us.

From there, we printed Free Hugs t-shirts and handed them out at the Brighton, MI 4th of July Parade. They were such a hit. The parade itself was a blur; all I remember seeing was people running back and forth and hugging each other down the main streets of Brighton. What an amazing concept and an amazing community, all with beginnings of a simple video shared by my brother. One of the greatest moments relating to this experience was when my brothers each donned a Free Hugs shirt for a photo.

Social Networks—Facebook in Real Life: Insurance

Here's a great example of how a local insurance agent has used social media to his advantage. InSights hosted a social media presentation for a local Chamber of Commerce. In the audience was a gentleman who has been involved in the insurance industry for a number of years. He was planning some new marketing and planning to send a letter to his contact list. For many people this is a default marketing behavior. We've all heard the advice before, when you are ready to tell people about something new, go to your friends and family list and mail everybody a letter. This agent was getting ready to send out this letter, but he was having reservations about whether it was the right thing to do. He had about 700 names on his list, and he didn't feel quite right sending out the letter. He didn't want to cross a line with some people, and come across as a "salesperson." He didn't want to be the guy who sent them a letter just because he wanted to market his business to them. He had real relationships with these people and he didn't want them to be afraid he was trying to sell them something the next time they saw him coming.

Based on what he learned at the presentation, he left class and immediately started his Facebook account. Within about a week, he had reconnected with old friends from high school, college buddies, and people he knew in the local business community through organizations and networking events. He started to follow the advice he'd just received in class. Instead of saying "Hey, I am really cool ... I can get you insurance at a great price," he used his wall in a very smart way. He started saying things like, "I am working late at the office today," "I just saved money for one of my clients," and "It's a great day to be a small business owner." Soon people were asking, "What are you doing working late today?" and "How are you saving your clients money?"

Those questions gave him permission to share more information. He could tell people, "I am an insurance agent. I own my firm here in Michigan, and I work really hard to help my customers save money." It wasn't long before people started saying, "Why don't you quote my insurance, It is coming up for renewal," and "Oh, really! Could you look at this for me? "These folks were already over the traditional barrier to doing business with someone new, because they had an existing relationship. This agent capitalized on new media. Instead of sending out that letter, he used his Facebook profile to expand his ABC List and let people know what he was doing. What was the beauty of this? He didn't have to sell a thing. He connected with people in a genuine way, focusing on the relationship first. Through this effort he was able to share "this is who I am, this is what I am doing, and here I am if you would like to do business with me." The results were fantastic. In about two weeks, he had prepared 18-20 quotes (which for a two week period and a new marketing effort was a great success!) By using social media and using it in a smart way, he was able to get people interested, intrigued and it led to great things for him.

One of the most challenging aspects of social media is how to measure the ROI (return on investment.) In the case of the insurance agent, the investment was some time and no money. The return on his time, both in learning social media and participating in it, was huge. Consider the alternative. Seven hundred letters could have been sent out; with an average direct mail return rate of between one and three percent, he could have expected between seven and 21 requests for quotes. Add to this the costs and time involved in creating the letter, putting the mailing together, adding postage, and running to the post office. The return in this case speaks for itself: 18-20 quotes with no financial investment and a growing and more robust social presence. We'd say that's a good return.

It is important to remember to set measurable ways to recognize your ROI. You can measure how many people call for quotes based on a marketing campaign. It can also be how many visitors spend time on your website or Facebook Page. Even more importantly, you can see how many people visit your website by way of your Facebook profile or business page. Once you define some measurables, for examples "I want to get this number to my website, this many coming from Twitter, and this many from Facebook." You can now check the demographics. You can also begin to redefine your efforts based on what you can observe from the statistic. You can determine your impact from posting at various times of the day. When you begin to understand how people are motivated and responding to your marketing, you will see traction in your social media strategy.

Favorites of our Marketing Club

We asked the question: What is your Favorite Tic-Tac Toe Square?

Dave Broadworth, Real Living Tremaine Real Estate: Social Networks!

Facebook is an easy way to get the word out. Twitter has grown considerably and can be used to bring people to any place on the internet. Periscope is a new tool that I am using to create awareness and quick tours of new homes that I bring to the market. When writing a blog, I also tweet out multiple times with links to the blog, and that brings in visitors. I've also found in real estate, I can't do enough videos. I am finally starting to capture even more images and have discovered that videos draw in more people than my words ever did.

Jackie Rendall, Rendall's Certified Cleaning Services: TLC—Think Like your Customer

One of my favorite marketing squares is "Thinking Like a Customer" because it goes beyond what you'd think.

Thinking like a customer helps you put yourself in a client's shoes. It really has nothing to do with your business! It only involves what your current or potential client actually thinks when trying to choose a business. How they would find a business. Where they would start looking. How they should choose where to go shopping.

Another square I like is the "Alliances" square. It made me think outside the box about other people and businesses that I might be connected with, just by having a very similar target audience.

InSights Community's marketing group doesn't focus on just "marketing." Rather, you are thinking about everything around marketing. It's hard to describe! I believe it has helped me grow not only as a business person, but grow as a better person in general.

John Pullum, Motivational Speaker and TV Host: Target Audience

All the squares are important so it is difficult to choose just one square. It's like making a cake and forgetting the flour, eggs, milk...

The Target Audience square is really important. If you don't know who your customers are, then how can you sell to people that you don't know or even where they are? You can't.

Picture your customer and every possible detail about them. If you can't picture them, you really need this square. You might be surprised on who your target audience is.

All the other squares are equally important. If you know and have an audience, you have to have all your squares in order to keep them. Now as I write more and really think about it, maybe the target audience square should be last? If you don't know "you," your "home," how your customers think etc., your audience won't be there. Can I say all 9 squares are my favorite? It is like saying which of my children is my favorite. I can't pick just one.

Christian Tombers, Motivational Speaker and Sales Training Consultant: YOU

It all starts with *you* (or me)

> My attitude
> My beliefs
> My contacts
> My resources
> My goals, wishes, dreams

If your thinking isn't in the right place, you won't see opportunities, possibilities and solutions.

The results and content of other squares is totally influenced by you, the person who comes up with the ideas, concepts, lists, assumptions, beliefs, habits, process.

Michelle Warden[53], Organic Chicken Wrangler: You—Understanding your Why

Developing and understanding the why of what I want to do. Indeed, what I do. I raise organic chickens. Yet more than that; developing an understanding of what motivates me in life and what I want to do on my next adventure.

Chad Warden[54], Craftsman: You and Target Audience

Ask the Universe: As I learned about Tic-Tac-Toe Marketing, I learned the power of asking the universe for what I am looking for. I asked for higher end, kitchen remodel jobs, and the universe delivered. It didn't take a lot of work on my part. It was as if, once I had the thought, I just started bumping into people who said, "'you know what I am looking for? "I am looking for someone to do a spectacular kitchen remodeling job. You wouldn't do that, would you?" It was as easy as that and I am booking high end kitchen remodel jobs every time I turn around! This stuff works!

Rita Long, Rita Long Art: Energy Signature

One of my favorite marketing squares is the "Energy Signature" square. It made me realize that *who* I am is more important than what I say. Who I am. Just who I am! And that made me

---

[53] Married,

[54] To each other.

focus on showing the world who I am and making sure my life is congruent in all areas.

Strategic Alliances:

This square inspired me to look beyond the typical marketing techniques. I have begun to talk to realtors who can refer home buyers to my website and my work. I am also contacting interior designers who could lead people to my work, as possibilities for decorating with their clients.

Scott Rendall, Rendall's Certified Cleaning Services: TLC—Think Like your Customer

My favorite tic-tac-toe square is "Think Like my Clients" because it really helped to sift down my previous favorite square which was "Target Market." TLC showed me that there is *much* more to knowing important stuff about the clients *I want* to work for.

Monica Tombers, Rosel's Chandeliers: Energy Signature

Where does motivation come from? Motivation is that energy that comes from a personal truth. This truth is not always obvious. It can even be close to impossible to specify and sometimes even harder to accept. In our Marketing Mastermind Group it took everyone in the room to help me understand that my main motivation is maintaining the legacy of the business' founders (my parents.) Making a living and having fun with tools and trinkets are not part of Energy Signature, it's the deep down conviction about how the product is designed, done up, and delivered.

Katie Curtis, Ask the Pool Guy: YOU

This is always my favorite square to do. It is interesting to look at where I am in life. I don't know that I can point to any one change, but many little changes emerge, as I always get inspired by this square. By doing, and re-doing, the tic–tac-toe board has helped me hone *me* and what I am doing.

Ron Cude, Legendary Escapes: Everything!

I started coming to marketing meetings just to see what it was about. I keep coming because I learn and take away so much. Group members, from more than one type of business, talk about ways to make their businesses more successful. The next week they come back and report success on whatever the idea was.

Something I've learned from the group is the way I look at my future: anything is possible. I have gained confidence in doing things my way and doing the why. I have been using things I have learned in this group when I think about life and why I do things.

Facebook Engagement Strategies

Post at least once a day – automating your blog is great, and then you need to share an additional post that doesn't automate from your blog. [55]

Write your posts in everyday language rather than technical jargon and acronyms.

Use proper grammar, punctuation and style. Do not shorten your post too much or write as if you are texting—gr8, u 2, or c u later are not going to set a good impression. Btw, do you know what they all mean?

Post when your audience is likely to see it or when most of your friends are on. Typically, this is going to be evenings and weekends. You can watch this by checking how many people are available for chat at certain times of the day.

Include a picture (thumbnail) with your link to posts – especially when content comes from your blog. We are visual, we want to see pictures.

Visit YouTube regularly and find something fun to share.

Respond back to every comment that you get. If someone takes the time to say "I thought about

---

[55] BufferApp.com is a (current in 2015) resource to automate content from around the web to drip out to your social media accounts via a preset schedule.

you." Take the time to say "I appreciate you" back.

New to Facebook? Try These Activities:

- ✓ Visit Daily/15 Minutes
- ✓ "Like" other pages
- ✓ Comment on posts from other pages
- ✓ Comment on friend's notes
- ✓ Comment on every response to your posts

Profile – *it's personal*

- ✓ set a goal for your # status updates/day/week
- ✓ make sure your profile shows Your smiling face!
- ✓ Share your blog posts via your profile with a service like BufferApp

Facebook Business Page Strategies

- ✓ Set a goal for your # status updates/day/week
- ✓ Use a PLOGO as your page logo picture (Photo/Logo Combo)
- ✓ Increase likes by promoting to friends
- ✓ Encourage friends to invite their friends to "like" your page.
- ✓ Be ORIGINAL!

If you have a business that has a page on Facebook, you'll quickly find out that people need a reason to find you, and to "like" you (which substitutes for the old terminology of becoming a "fan.") The lingo is different, but the concept is the same. You'll need some creative ways to influence the "liking" of your page.

One of the quickest ways to get a few "likes" of your page is to use the "suggest to friends" link directly under the logo (hopefully you've included a plogo (photo/logo) combo in the box. This will send out a message to all your friends suggesting they like your page. If they don't click in, don't over abuse this tool. Once or twice is fine. Then move onto one of the other methods listed below.

Embed the Facebook Widget on your Websites

Put the quick link to your Facebook Page or Profile on your website.

Invite your Email Subscribers to engage with you on Facebook

As we developed our Pool Guy persona, one of the places people could go was to our Facebook page to ask questions and see what we were working on. We shared this on our website, and in our newsletters for specific products and services. People feel comfortable messaging on Facebook, so make sure to share and monitor posts and messages coming your way!

When you add the Facebook Logo or a badge to your newsletter, and have the hyperlink go directly to your page. There is nothing worse than hitting a Facebook button that just heads over to Facebook.com without getting us to the final destination.

Add to your Outgoing Email Signature

Just as you would include a link to your personal profile in your email signature (or if you are close to your friend limit), include a link to your business page in your email.

Use the Power of Photos!

Take photos at events and have everyone tag themselves in the photos. Now your contacts, and their contacts will see what you are up to. (Make sure to set the album to public, and start on your page for the best impact!)

If you sell cookies or cupcakes, take a photo and let people know the first person to tag each treat can stop in and pick it up for themselves. Share a picture of something related to your business and follow the same strategy. An amusement park also used this technique by taking an aerial photo of the rides, giving a free ride to each person who tagged the ride first. *That's a whole lot of WIIFM!*

Try some Facebook Ads

Start small, and boost your likes by using a social ad. To get to the advertising section, scroll to the foot of any page inside Facebook and click the link at the very bottom that says "Advertising." From there, it should walk you right through the steps to create your ad for your target market.

Run a Contest

Get creative with ways to have people like your page to be entered for cool prizes. This one should be quick and easy! A car dealership ran a cutest baby contest where users emailed in photos, and the picture with the most likes at the end of the contest won. The cool part, a voter had to like the page in order for the like an individual photo function was possible. Get parents encouraging people to vote for their page—it works wonders!

Link to Twitter

Link your Twitter account to your Facebook fan page and automatically post your Facebook content to Twitter. You can edit what gets posted, choosing from Status Updates, Photos, Links, Notes and Events.

Show it on your Stuff

Look at every piece of print media that you have for your business that we fondly refer to as "the stuff." When you choose your username for the various sites, be as consistent as possible. Once people know your call sign they can find you wherever they look.

Display a Places icon at your Business

If your business is run from a physical location, share the fact that you are a Places location on Facebook (or Foursquare) so they can check in from their mobile phone. Let them know the WIIFM so they can join and show your staff to receive their incredible incentive offer!

Add a Link on your Personal Profile

In the "write something about yourself" section of your personal profile, add the link to your page. This is especially important if you are close to your "friend" limit, so people can still be in contact with you.

Be sure to format the URL with http://www.yourwebite.com; it will not be clickable with just the www's.

Use the Share Button

The Share button is all over Facebook and is a very handy feature. Periodically go to your fan page, scroll toward the bottom left column and click the "Share+" button. Encourage the people who like your page to do the same.

Add a compelling comment along the lines of exciting news, recent changes, special incentives, etc., happening on your fan page and invite your friends to join if they haven't already. If you'd like to Share content from the web on to your *fan page* and multiple profile sites, we highly recommend using the BufferApp.

Use the @ Mention

As long as you're a fan of your own fan page, you can "@ tag" it on your own personal profile wall.

From time to time, let your friends know about something happening on your fan page by writing a personal status update that includes tagging your fan page with the @ tag.

Engaging your Audience on Twitter

- ✓ Be concise, and save room for people to add the RT so they can easily share your tweet ("RT @ [your handle] ") 120 Characters is a good length to allow for the space to RT

- ✓ Use keywords without being overly technical in your tweets
- ✓ When you have loyal followers, ask for RTs and Comments!
- ✓ Tweet with full words; maybe I don't know what the abbreviation is, so the content will be lost on me
- ✓ Tweet at the right time to engage your audience—mid morning for business posts, evenings/weekends for inspirational and entertainment based posts
- ✓ If applicable, use words like insights, analysis, and opinion. Posts with these words get more views and links.
- ✓ Write to your audience, and run it through the you/me filter
- ✓ People love bullet lists of information, 10 tips to a better...5 steps to...Add your commentary to posts you RT, "awesome, check it out" or "You will want to read this!"

5 Tips for Engaging on Twitter

Plan—identify why you want to use Twitter; once you have a goal, you can work out a Twitter plan. Otherwise you might use all of your time surfing and playing, without getting closer to your purpose. Are you hoping to connect with friends and family? Do you want to promote your brand or blog? Do you want to meet new people? Use it for networking? Keep tabs on your brand, image, or company? All of the above, and more, are great reasons to use Twitter.

Tweet!—Jump in with both feet. You will build a great Twitter network through your activity. If you post interesting things, people will be inclined to follow you. Share useful information, fun facts, and add some of your personality. That's what it's all about! Give people a reason to follow you. Be interesting, rather than self-promoting.

Follow—Follow other Twitter users. Follow people because of their interesting posts. Target conversations near you if you are looking to grow in your geographic area. Expand your reach if you have a farther-reaching goal.

React—Reply, Retweet, and have those conversations! Reach out, share information, and let others know that you find them interesting. Asking questions is a great way to get some answers! Respond to others. Use the reply feature or the @username to have those two sided conversations.

Play Nice—Practice restraint and Twitter Etiquette. Avoid spam. Promote content that is interesting. Don't bring in the band and banners declaring yourself the next best thing since sliced bread[56].

---

[56] It was approximately 100 years ago when Otto Frederick Rohwedder of Davenport, Iowa, USA invented the first loaf-at-a-time bread-slicing machine.

Organic Marketing ™

Insert your personality, interests, and yes promote yourself, but do it in balance with everything else. Share others' links and information. Be the person at the party that listens as well as they talk.

10 Great Social Media Status Updates

You've been sitting in front of your computer for what seems like an eternity.[57] You want to write a status update, but you are not sure what to do. Here are 10 great ideas for social media status updates. (We tend to write about Facebook, since that's our favorite site, though these ideas apply to any of the social media sites).

- ✓ Do a friend shout out: *@enternamehere, thanks for the help with* (project, service, advice)
- ✓ Talk about something amazing that happened in your day.
- ✓ Share a random quote. (Don't be surprised that some readers will check on your accuracy.)[58]

---

[57] Or at least that is what the book's editor feels like. Not that it has not been an absolute pleasure!

[58] The US Postal Service recently put out a stamp with a quote that was not from the person depicted. Twitter can be a great fact checking service. Of course it's free and totally worth the price.

✓ Find a post from a blog that you enjoy, and share it with your friends.

✓ Find a blog post from YOUR blog that you enjoy and share it with your friends.

✓ Head over to YouTube, search for something cool—the most popular video of the week, your favorite song, or how to do something—and share it with your friends. Not just anything – something you were happy to find.

✓ Stop by Twitter and check out trending topics. Find a post and share it on your wall

✓ Mention an event that you are going to: *@namehere, can't wait to see you at the (event name here) on Thursday. Let's catch up.* If it's a meetup event or on Facebook and the public is invited, share the link so more friends can RSVP.

✓ Ask for help: I'm working on updating my social media status, what is the best status update that you've seen shared on Facebook?

✓ Ask for a referral: *I'm looking for a good drywaller, who do you recommend."* We suggest that you only post this type of inquiry if you really have a need – if you get in the habit of asking for something different every day, people might begin to wonder what you are up to and why you need so many drywallers.

Video Production Hints

Authentic Voice—Share your authentic message, in your authentic voice. Over-projection or over production is not a good idea. Ensure that you project so that the device can record you evenly and your viewers can hear you. Avoid artificial accents or over exaggeration. Just your normal, awesome, wonderful self will do. Or to paraphrase Katherine Hepburn's advice to the up and coming actor, Richard Burton, "Don't act...speak the words!"

Sound Quality—*"Can you hear me now?"* or is there too much background noise? Do pay attention to your surroundings. Lavalier microphones (like you see newscasters and interviewers using) are available at very low prices to get you started. Using a windsock or some type of windbreak can also make a huge difference. Sometimes a directional mike is needed to isolate your brilliant presentation from the rest of the crowd.

Editing your Videos

With all the advances in video technology, everybody has the ability to be a movie maker. Good stuff is the good content; no matter if the lighting's a bit off, someone misspoke, or the cat walked by. While this authentic style is effective, don't overlook editing. No every uncut vlog (video blog) or off-the-cuff introduction is worthy of posting. Watchers have the ability to click away if something does not please them, so their attention span is much shorter than it used to be. Good editing is the key. No special effects are needed, just a bit of good judgment on what should and should NOT go into a video.

Good: Dialogue and/or images pertaining to the topic.

Not-Good: Wild filming that transitions from one room to another, irrelevant graphics or slides, garbled or unintelligible speech, or rambling completely off topic, unless it's amusing or will serve to make a point.

You don't need *Final Cut* or other expensive editing software. Most computers come with an easy to use program built in, no downloads necessary. (On your Mac, look for iMovie; on Windows, open Windows Movie Maker. If you don't have these, try the online editing software available in your YouTube account.)

The idea is to create a *video strategy* to engage with your customers by using video in creative ways that will strengthen your brand and allow you to have a bit of fun in the process. Part of that strategy is deciding if or how you will measure the ROI or Return on Investment. This is nearly impossible, so focus on what really counts. We found that for our company the number of "Likes" and "Views" really don't matter. The number of contacts from compatible clients does. We are not looking for quantity but for qualification.

Just in case you think that you will quickly run out of ideas for videos, let's look at some specific ways to use videos to engage your audience:

Communicate your Ideas—Share your message on video and it's sure to be listened to. Share announcements for events, product launches and more!

Produce Case Studies—Share case studies of clients. What was the issue that you helped to solve? What are the steps involved in working with you? What are some of the tangible and measurable results?

Share behind the Scenes—Use video to show behind the scenes at your company. If you show what goes on day to day, people can get a better feel for your company and how it works. We love to know how you do what you do, and show everything from the order process, to manufacturing and more. These don't have to be professionally produced, but they do need to be interesting and fun.

Think about what your customers would like the insider view of and share it via online channels. Use empathy to decide if you will show any bloopers or irregularities. Being transparent is one thing. Embarrassing a person or demeaning a product is not a part of your Certain Way. Now about those proprietary processes and secret sauce ingredients... if you show them, they won't be. If you approach this as we have, you'll become even more creative as you teach others your methods—so don't be afraid to share, though we do realize some secret sauce recipes should be kept in the vault.

(Your Name Here) TV—Set a schedule and record a regular "TV segment" to broadcast online. It's a great way to communicate with your audience. When you watch someone regularly you feel like you get to know them, you recognize them by face and by voice. Hmmm, wouldn't it be great if your customers all recognized you, and looked forward to your program every week?

There is another great side effect of videos. As your customers get to know you, they will start reading all of your written correspondence with your voice including your timbre, your inflections, your confidence, and even your smile.

Mini Documentary—Create a story about your company, product, service, or event. Share a behind the scenes look at filming your videos that you are sharing. Document the process of working with a client, share your thoughts and combine several of the elements on this list for a unique look at your story.

News and Commentary—Use a video to offer commentary on trending industry topics or news and share your video via your social media sites. This will help your clients understand that you are aware of your industry and pro-active about sharing.

Screencast—to demonstrate a point or instructions for how to do something online, create a video using screen casting capabilities. This is a great way to record instructions and

FAQ answers for people using your website or product.

Dear Diary/Philosophy—Tell a story, talking to the camera and sharing an inside look at your company values, motivation or the story of how the company got its start. You can also offer simple and short tip videos, answer commonly asked questions, or give an update of something trending in the news.

Reach Out—Share a profound video message about a cultural trend. Share a "what if" perspective. Present something with a warm and fuzzy component. You'll gain respect for sharing things that people feel an emotional connection to, especially if the message resonates with your company culture and Energy Signature.

Product Tours—give a tour of your product via video, especially if it's an online product. What if it's not? A walk through of a live demonstration of your offline product can be a lot of fun as well. Show real people using the product and seeing the benefits.

Training—Video sessions are a great option when live training would be cost prohibitive or unnecessary. You can perform them live or you can record for future playback. Try to create short segments so viewers don't have to sit through 60 minutes to get to the content they need. 20, 10, or even 5 minute sections with descriptive titles make it easier to digest new information and pinpoint items for review.

Client Reviews—Turn the camera on your clients and ask them to create videos in response to yours or as a product review for your product or service. Some will be super excited to share and you can capitalize on their enthusiasm. Real people with real opinions, we might be on to something here.

Yes, you will find the camera shy and tongue-tied. Promise them that you will not share the video if they do not like the result. Yet, should they squawk, follow *Your Certain Way,* respect their request, keep your promise, and try again another day. (It might just be that it was a bad hair day or even a no hair day.)

Interviews—Interview your customers, interview your employees, take a note from fun video creation and try to interview yourself. This offers a great way to share your message with a Q/A format that people can tune into. With a little video editing you can even present point and counterpoint.

A quick word of caution, you would rather share good information as an amateur videographer than not share anything because you are intimidated that it is too complicated to create.

Interviews with Influencers—who are some of the key people within your industry? Interview them. Share a video that they've been in, to help make a point. If there is not a video out there, ask them. Flattery will get you everywhere. You will be amazed how much support you will get if you ask to showcase them or their world.

Have some fun with it!—Some of the best videos that companies share are when the staff is having fun. Don't try to be serious all the time. Allow some of your fun company culture to come through. This allows for showcasing what you do, and will put your audience at ease so they don't feel like they are watching an infomercial.

Pixar loves to show how much fun their teams have creating animated movies. You can find these clips on their DVDs under Extras. And, oh, by the way, award winning products are being created by passionate people that love what they are doing, even when it goes into unpaid overtime.

Fun fact: Forrester Research[vii] shares that "A website with a video is 53 times more likely to come up on the first page result on Google than the exact same page without video."

Where to Share your Videos

Email—Send a video in an email. Just make sure you send a brief description so that people feel okay to click on it. Some email programs allow you to embed a video (this works if you are using HTML formats such as Microsoft Outlook or Mozilla Thunderbird). You won't have such luck with some web-based programs.

YouTube—Share your short video on YouTube (typically 10 minutes or less). YouTube is a great place to gain exposure; it is searched almost as much as regular search engines and is a great way to have your information found. So far search engines can't see into your video to "read" keywords and content (although that feature is coming), so make sure to include a good description of what the video is about, including your keywords. In some cases, a transcript of the video is a great idea to include too. It's another way for your viewers to share your message.

Facebook—Videos shared on Facebook are likely to show up on someone else's news feed, and as an added bonus they begin to auto play to capture more attention. Think about using Facebook to share a company video, testimonial, and anything fun and exciting that you are up to.

Videos can be uploaded directly into Facebook or linked over from YouTube. In some cases, you might want to put your video in both places. Know your strategy and create a strong video library. Users love videos, so it's extremely beneficial for businesses to continue to add to their library, and make it searchable.

The blog *All Facebook* recently reported, "Nearly 47 million people in the U.S. watched videos on Facebook in February 2011. That puts the site in fourth place on the comScore Video Metrix ranking, two spots higher than it ranked in January." For July 2015 ComScore posted that "Google Sites, driven primarily by video viewing at *YouTube.com*, ranked as the top online video content property in July with 169.2 million unique viewers. *Facebook* ranked #2 with 89.4 million viewers..."

LinkedIn—LinkedIn's company pages make it possible for your company to add a video for your products and services. When you add a video clip to your page, your visitors are highly likely to click play to see what you are all about.

Skype—Use Skype to do video calling via your computer, iPhone or other capable mobile phone. Group video calls can be a lot of fun and allow for screen sharing with your associates.

Livestream or Ustream or Periscope—Offer days and times when people can get online live with you and your company for a real-time discussion. Record the session for future playback, and post it on your blog or a landing page.

Apple's FaceTime—Apple's FaceTime has created a new option for video calls, on a Mac, iPhone or iPad2. Salesforce.com even has plans to use FaceTime as a way to provide face-to-face customer support.

Social Relationship on Twitter

Twitter is a micro-blog. You have 140 or fewer characters to get your message across. It functions like a blog, except for the size, so you have to be very quick and concise in telling your story.

Allan shares his understanding of Twitter.

"When I first caught wind of Twitter, I didn't understand anything about it and the first "tweet" (that message you send out is called a tweet) I read said, "Just got out of the shower ... heading off to work." I read that on my computer screen and said, "So what? Why do I care? What do I want to know that for?" The next one that came through said, "I was driving to work today and, boy, the sunrise was beautiful." Again, it made no sense to me. I put Twitter on the shelf for a while and thought, well, I must have missed it; there is nothing there.

Slowly, I started realizing the psychology behind Twitter. Let's go back to the first tweet. "I took a shower." That's probably a good sign that this person has some good habits. The second thing was, "I'm heading off to work." Well that little statement, "I'm heading off to work," means this person has a job. If they have a job, they probably have money. If they have money, they might be willing to buy my service. I learned a lot about this person: got good hygiene (that's great), but more importantly, they are working, they are active, and they are a potential client. So that is when I got re-involved with Twitter and recognized it is as a huge tool to learn those snippets of things about people and share your message with an awful lot of people with one post."

Twitter differs from some of the other social media sites in that you don't have to give permission for people to follow you. Within Twitter, there are followers and there are people who you are following. When you first sign up for a Twitter account your numbers are zero; zero followers and zero people following you.

Twitter Philosophy

A key to building a following on Twitter is to stand out from the crowd.

Al's persona on Twitter is philosophical: questions of the day, passing on information, just getting people to think about who and what they are and where they are in their busy lives and how they can slow down and calm down. Mixed in with that are book suggestions, blog posts, sending people to the website, and getting people involved and engaged with what we are. Using that balance has created interest for Al, and as he's discovered, if you create interest, you get traction.

Twitter is texting on steroids. By sending out a message with the click of a button, it goes to many, many, many people. The best part is that if your message is good people will either RT (retweet) or share your message with their friends. If you are consistently good, or someone is interested in finding out more, a well-designed Twitter account will lead people to your online home, your website.

Create messages that are unique and interesting so that people want to visit your online home. The easiest way to do this is to have a link on your profile. Another way is to automate your blog posts to your Twitter feed and create interesting headlines that compel people to click on the link to read more.

The next step in your Twitter strategy is to find interesting people to follow. You can follow people in a specific industry, for example. If you are in a certain geographic location, you can narrow down the scope of the people you follow based on their location. When you first start following people, make sure that you are looking for people who tweet with some frequency. People who are not posting very often are not sharing much new information that you can learn and share. If you follow active people on Twitter, you will be able to share your message with others effectively. You will also learn a whole lot by paying attention to what other people have to say.

LinkedIn Profile Building

When building your LinkedIn profile, include a professional headshot. Make sure that you have completed your work history, the schools that you have gone to, and the different groups and organizations that you have been involved with. We know, through our work with professional recruiters, that they often scan a resume from the bottom to the top. Make sure that you spend as much time making the end of your profile as interesting, relevant and informational as the top. Use keywords well. Focus on the experiences that will be sought after and, in LinkedIn, don't be afraid to go into extensive detail. It will help you with long-tail keyword searches and the people trying to find you will appreciate it.

Once you have your profile up and running, you will want to take some time to research the question and answer section of LinkedIn, as well as look for different groups and associations that you can join or that you can belong to. In LinkedIn, your sphere of influence is based on the connections that you have. It is also based on the groups and the associations that you have built within the LinkedIn system. Even if you are not connected with somebody one-on-one, if you have a group in common or if you have become involved in a discussion, the door is now open for you to make that new connection.

One of the best ways to use LinkedIn is to strategically look for people with whom you want to build a relationship. LinkedIn is not as much about getting to the end user who will buy your product or service as it is about connecting with people who know the people who will buy your product or service. Keep that in mind when you are making connections.

Strategies for LinkedIn

Target select companies that you would like to do business with, research the people who work there, and make a point of setting "Get to Know You" appointments. These are not sales calls! Simply make connections. I found you on

LinkedIn. I would like to get to know you better. We might have something in common.

Those "Getting to Know You" conversations can be online, via telephone, or best, in person. A great approach is to let people know the reason you are seeking the connection. Share that you think you could be great resources for each other in the future. Put your prospect at ease by letting them know that you are not expecting anything from them right now, but consider them a valuable connection to possibly help each other in the future.

When we are in the process of building relationships, trying to sell our product, or market our product, common ground with that person sitting on the other side of the table is what links us together. "I found you on LinkedIn," is a type of permission for that person to at least give you a few moments of conversation. This is a huge tool if used properly. If you are calling on a company and you are looking for someone in the HR Department, if you don't have a name, your likelihood of getting through is relatively slim. Find a direct contact via LinkedIn, your odds of getting in the door go up dramatically. It is easier to get an appointment with a person than with a title.

LinkedIn: Research

Within LinkedIn, one of the most powerful tools is the ability to research people. LinkedIn groups the information and makes it readily available for you to find out how many people work at a company, who the direct contacts are, and how you can communicate with them. It is a great place to find work if you are looking for a job or know someone looking for employment.

The key, though, is in understanding that you need credibility; if you lack credibility, people will be reluctant to be involved with you. LinkedIn makes gaining credibility very simple, by asking for and giving recommendations. Recommend people who you have done business with. Recommend people who you know. If you tell the world about this person, it is third-party validation, and the more you can do that, the more likely people are to do that for you as well. That credibility factor is huge. The more we know about a person and the more we know that someone else talks about that person in such a way, the stronger the relationship will be.

Automation

With the social media sites (Facebook, LinkedIn, and Twitter), it is possible to automate your blog posts to feed out to your various profiles. Automatically sending your Facebook blog entry, for example, to Twitter is a great idea. There are free tools on the internet to allow you to "Fill a funnel." That means that you can submit several posts at one time but schedule them to post slowly on the various media. This allows you (or others) to create a series of posts at one time – a much more efficient way to handle and keep track of all the posting.

Keep in mind: make sure that your tweets (and other posts) are interesting. If everything that you tweet about is business promotion, leading people back to your website, people are going to tune you out because they are not going to see you as having new, fresh, relevant information that is beneficial to them.

A strong information campaign, automatically feeding the various outlets, is best with a varied content mix. Add some personal insights, interesting ideas, and great resources for people to find, so that you are interesting...which you are.

Now that we've given you some ideas, head out there and start to engage with us!

About the Authors

Allan Curtis aka *Ask the Pool Guy*, Sandi Maki aka *Ask the Pool Girl*

Allan Curtis is the co-owner and Designer/Builder at Legendary Escapes. He didn't start out in love with the pool industry, though that is exactly where he finds himself now. A 28-year pool industry veteran, Al received the Master of Design Award in 2013 from *Pool and Spa News.* Starting with the basics of swimming pool design he has pushed the limits of both himself and the industry, leading innovation and pioneering the Hybrid Swimming Pool Build process. Al and team have expanded into a boutique building company, specializing in artistic and themed backyard escapes. A philosophy guy at heart, the connection with the homeowners is the most important aspect of one of Al's pools, and his portfolio speaks for itself.

Al maintains a high industry profile as a public speaker and networker, regularly presenting at the International Pool Show and other industry events. A published author, Al is also a regular contributor to *AQUA Magazine* and a frequent speaker and consultant on organic marketing for business owners. His online alter-ego *Ask the Pool Guy* has garnered him industry-wide recognition, and he has a solid social media base of 50K Twitter followers and a YouTube channel with 750+ videos. Al earned a BA in physics, a background which helps inform his pool building technique. He lives in a 100+ year old farm house, enjoys antiquing to find interesting elements to his swimming pool themes, and enjoys fishing and spending time with his family, especially his daughters who have become an integral part of his swimming pool construction team.

Sandi Maki is the co-owner and marketing juggernaut of Legendary Escapes as well as a marketing consultant for business owners and the creator of the *Ask the Pool Guy* online persona. A published author, Sandi is a new contributor to *AQUA Magazine* with her Ask the Pool Girl alter ego, accomplished photographer and frequent podcaster, Sandi regularly consults with business owners on how to build and grow an organic marketing presence. With 100k+ Twitter followers and a strong presence on several social channels, Sandi has learned first-hand how to harness the power of digital marketing to leverage exposure and build a brand. She holds a BA in Psychology with a Business and Marketing emphasis. Sandi is the mother of two adorable (almost all grown-up) kids, and is always willing to listen, learn, share and grow. Her enthusiasm is infectious, and her work speaks for itself.

Legendary Escapes—Originally, a vinyl pool building and service company, Al Curtis and Sandi Maki have grown Legendary Escapes into a sought-after premium pool building company by relentlessly striving to refine the work they do, who they do it for, and how they go about it. In the process, they have also created a business support group (aka the Insights Clubhouse) where small business owners gather to share innovative thinking on creating businesses and lives in which they can truly express their passions and their Certain Way.

Additional Resources by your Authors

To enhance your Organic Marketing™ Plans start here:

Our Certain Way, the Building of a Legendary Pool Business (2015)

Organic Marketing™ Building Blocks and Follow Up:

Social Media Explained* (2009)
Social Media Strategies* (2010)
Blogging Explained*(2009)
Blogging Strategies*(2010)
Organic Marketing™ Explained* (2009)
Organic Marketing™ Advanced Strategies for Social Media* (2010)

*Audio CD

Pool Resources:

Ask the Pool Guy's Everyday Guide to Swimming Pools (2013)

Fun and Quirky Reads:

100 Marbles: How the Collective Mind, Gratitude and Masterminding Changed

our Lives – A Journey through the InSights Mastermind (2013)
Heavy Breathing Just Before Midnight & Fuzzy New Socks (2013)

Developing your Certain Way:

The Science of Getting Rich by Wallace D. Wattles (2014)
The Science of Being Well by Wallace D. Wattles (2014)
The Science of Being Great by Wallace D. Wattles (2014)
The Science of Getting Rich by Wallace D. Wattles Audio – as read by Sandi Maki* (2011) *Audio CD

InSights Certain Way:

The Culture of InSights* (2010) *Audio CD

Industry Specific:

3 Dimensional Relationship Marketing for Dentists & the Psychology of Social Media* (2011) *Audio CD

www.askthepoolguy.com
www.insights-group.com

End Notes

[i] Sinek, Simon. (2009). *Start with Why: How Great Leaders Inspire Everyone to Take Action*. Portfolio

[ii] Godin, Seth (2011). *Permission Marketing: Turning Strangers into Friends and Friends into Customers.* Simon & Schuster

[iii] Farber, Steve (2009). *Greater Than Yourself: The Ultimate Lesson of True Leadership.* Doubleday.

[iv] Godin, Seth (2008). *Tribes: We Need you to Lead Us.* Portfolio

[v] Knapp, Renee and Dorr, D (1985). Beyond the Color Explosion: The Color Key Program

[vi] IbisWorld Market Research on Swimming Pool Construction in the U.S., 2013.

[vii] "26 Ways to Engage With Customers Using Video." *Social Media Examiner RSS*. N.p., 05 Apr. 2011. Web. 27 Sept. 2015.